8/29

Youth Advisors' Handbook

Youth Advisors' Handbook

A Resource for YRUU Advisors

Second Edition

Shell Tain

Unitarian Universalist Association
Boston

Printed in the USA.

ISBN 1-55896-461-4

Cover design by Kathryn Sky-Peck
Text design by WordCrafters

10 9 8 7 6 5 4 3 2
06 05

Acknowledgments

Many people across the continent contributed to this handbook when it was first created, some directly and some through their past work with youth. Our thanks to the following individuals who have not just contributed to this handbook but have continued to learn, grow, and stand for youth: Jory Agate for her editing; Laila Ibrahim for the history of YRUU; Jaco B. ten Hove for insights on youth worship; Adam Leite for his information on youth group leadership; Meg Riley for her perspective on the role of an advisor; Wayne Arnason for writing the first *Youth Advisors' Handbook,* and Anne Fleming, Rob Cavenaugh, and Rachel Reed for their support and assistance.

Jesse Jaeger served as the developmental editor for this second edition, and Joseph Lyons and Marjorie Bowens-Wheatley contributed new material. Youth Office staff Megan Tideman, Mimi LaValley, and Ethan Field provided important updated material. Jacqui James, Tony Brumfield, and Melanie Griffin provided valuable critique of the manuscript. Curriculum development assistant Barbara Gifford provided valuable editorial support.

Contents

Introduction

This handbook is a working tool for youth group advisors of Young Religious Unitarian Universalists (YRUU). It is both an introduction to advising and a resource for your continuing use.

There is no one right way to serve a youth group. There are many types of groups in congregations with varying needs, and different styles of advising will be appropriate for each group. As an advisor, you will need to adjust to your particular situation—and to keep adjusting as the youth in your group grow and the congregation's needs change. The *Youth Advisors' Handbook* offers models from a variety of youth group settings, raises questions, examines issues, and lists resources so that you can decide what is best for you. The final chapter, "How to Support Youth Advisors," is addressed to religious professionals and offers advice on recruiting and supporting youth advisors. Make sure the minister, religious educator, and anyone else responsible for youth programming at your congregation read it!

Although numerous types of youth group programs exist across the continent, the best programs are youth-centered, youth-focused, and youth-led. If you treat youth as competent and capable, they will respond in kind.

Adults choose to become youth group advisors for a variety of reasons and are rewarded in many ways for their gifts of time, concern, interest, and effort. Perhaps the best reward is the knowledge that you have helped young people to learn about and express themselves, grow in confidence, and discover abilities they never imagined they had.

Youth advising has been likened to providing the chalice for the fire of youth. As advisors, we hold the group in our protection and allow the individual flames of its members to ignite and dance within that protected space. Please join us. You will find many questions, some answers, untold rewards, and the joy of getting to know people of genuine fire.

The UUA has a Youth Office in Boston to serve as a resource for youth and advisors. Staffed by a youth programs director, two to three YRUU program specialists (who serve one-year terms), and the Youth Office administrative assistant, the Youth Office helps coordinate and plan Youth Council, Steering Committee, and Youth Social Justice Council. It also publishes *Synapse* (the YRUU continental newsletter), maintains an extensive website (www.uua.org/yruu), and manages multiple electronic mailing lists. The Youth

Office staff is available to you as a resource for district advisor trainings, leadership development conferences, and youth program consultation. This is the place to call for ideas, comfort, support, and help. You can reach them at 617-948-4350 or yruu@uua.org.

YRUU and the Youth Advisor

Because different youth relate to different kinds of adults, people with a variety of personality types and talents are needed as youth group advisors. Whether you are an extrovert or introvert, analytical or imaginative, there is a place for you in Young Religious Unitarian Universalists (YRUU).

It is important for you to choose a place within YRUU in which you feel at home. Trying to force yourself into an uncomfortable role will not serve you or the youth. After all, your primary function is to be a role model as an adult, as a human, and as a Unitarian Universalist.

Those of us involved with YRUU try to create many opportunities for youth. A group of youth and advisors listed the following goals at a Pacific Central District meeting. We try to provide

- an opportunity for youth to experience their own power
- an opportunity for youth to congregate freely and explore ideas
- an opportunity for youth to feel fully loved and accepted by other youth and advisors
- a confidential and safe place
- an alternative to the restrictions of home and school
- an opportunity for religious, personal, and artistic expression in a non-judgmental environment

- a place to deal with gender issues, where roles are up for grabs
- a way to recognize youth involvement in the denomination
- a forum for exploring religious ideas and religious identity
- support for leadership abilities and the opportunity to build leadership skills
- an opportunity for community building
- a unique forum for self-expression and self-discovery
- a ministry to liberal youth
- a place to share laughter and tears
- outreach beyond the denomination
- a place where all can express different opinions
- a place where all can be genuinely who they are

YRUU is all these things and more: it can be anything participants wish to make it. YRUU's potential is as great as the participants' creativity, motivation, and willingness to work.

YRUU History

Young Religious Unitarian Universalists grew out of Liberal Religious Youth (LRY), which was created in 1953 after the the Unitarian and the Universalist youth movements merged. In 1969, the youth leaders of Liberal Religious Youth called for autonomy from the Unitarian Universalist Association. With an endowment and continued funding from the UUA Board of Trustees, Liberal Religious Youth became a separate organization.

In 1976, the UUA Board of Trustees established the Special Committee on Youth Programs to evaluate youth programming. The Committee found that programs for youth were ineffective and inadequate, and recommended a continental dialogue between youth and adults in order to create more effective youth programming, along with an increased commitment from the denomination.

This continental dialogue took the form of two week-long conferences—"Common Ground" and "Common Ground: Coming of Age." Youth and adult representatives from all districts were present to shape the future of youth programming. Out of this process, Young Religious Unitarian Universalists was born on January 1, 1983. Liberal Religious Youth was dissolved and the remaining endowment given to YRUU.

YRUU had a difficult legacy to overcome in its early years. Many adults were distrustful of youth activities while many youth felt as if their independence had been undermined by the formation of YRUU.

In 1987 the Youth Council and the UUA Board requested a review of YRUU. The Five-Year Review Committee Report (1989) stated that youth involvement in programs, leadership, and the denomination had increased and had a positive effect on Unitarian Universalism. In 1995, the YRUU Youth Council again requested that the UUA review YRUU to see if it was still meeting its goals. The Youth Programs Review Committee reviewed the previous fifteen years of YRUU's existence and completed its report in June of 1997. The report, which examined all aspects of youth programming in the denomination, recommended, among other things, that YRUU needed to increase programming and resources for advisor training and support. In response, the UUA Board of Trustees established a task force to examine and make recommendations on youth advisor issues. The report also noted the increased demand by

youth for structured curricula. The fifteen-year report is available through the Youth Office and is a valuable resource for everyone involved in youth work.

The Organization of YRUU

YRUU is structured as a service organization. (See facing page.) While many youth are now involved in local, district, and continental YRUU programs, many more are involved in local congregations without connections to district or continental events. But whether a congregation's youth group calls itself YRUU or The Green Potatoes, the services of the YRUU and the UUA Youth Office are available to the group.

Youth Council, the governing body of continental YRUU, meets every summer. Each of the twenty UUA districts and sends a youth representative to Youth Council. There is also representation from Canadian youth, as well as several youth and adult at-large positions and a youth-of-color caucus. Youth Council is responsible for writing and updating the purposes and bylaws of continental YRUU and for making decisions regarding the organization's direction. Representatives use a consensus process to create and pass resolutions related to YRUU programming.

Past Youth Council decisions include changing the age range of continental YRUU, selecting a social action theme for the year, asking the UUA Board of Trustees to fund leadership development conferences, and declaring the value of eating coffee ice cream with Junior Mints. Youth Council decisions are binding only for the continental organization of YRUU and are not mandates to any particular district or congregation, although many decisions and policies made at Youth Council are adopted by individual districts.

The Youth Council elects a Steering Committee to carry out its decisions. Made up of nine youth and two adults (one of whom is a member of the UUA Board of Trustees), the Steering Committee meets four times a year and is responsible

YRUU Continental Structure

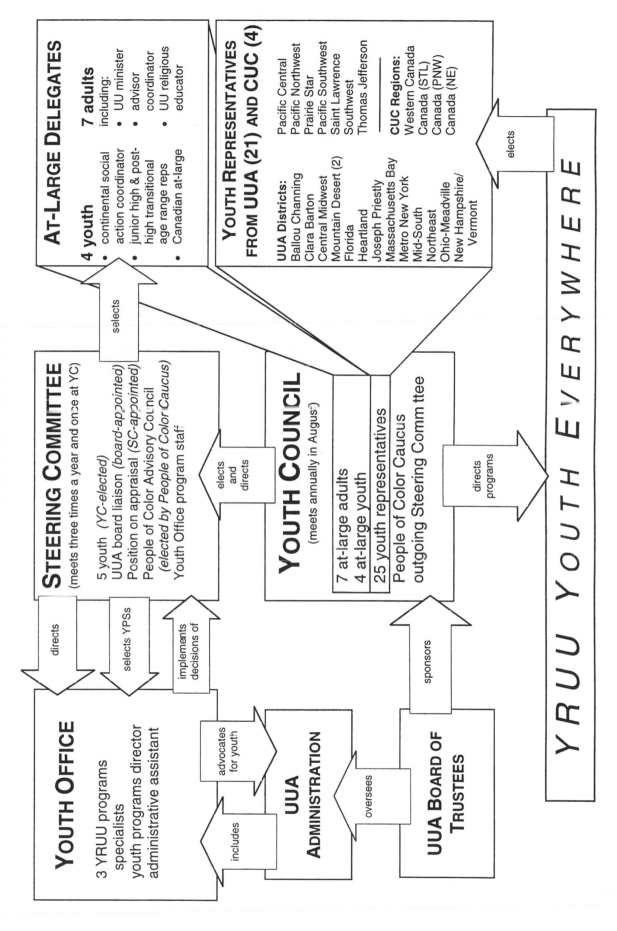

YRUU YOUTH EVERYWHERE

At-Large Delegates

4 youth
- continental social action coordinator
- junior high & post-high transitional age range reps
- Canadian at-large

7 adults
including:
- UU minister
- advisor coordinator
- UU religious educator

Youth Representatives from UUA (21) and CUC (4)

UUA Districts:
Ballou Channing
Clara Barton
Central Midwest
Mountain Desert (2)
Florida
Heartland
Joseph Priestly
Massachusetts Bay
Metro New York
Mid-South
Northeast
Ohio-Meadville
New Hampshire/Vermont
Pacific Central
Pacific Northwest
Prairie Star
Pacific Southwest
Saint Lawrence
Southwest
Thomas Jefferson

CUC Regions:
Western Canada
Canada (STL)
Canada (PNW)
Canada (NE)

Steering Committee
(meets three times a year and once at YC)

5 youth (YC-elected)
UUA board liaison (board-appointed)
Position on appraisal (SC-appointed)
People of Color Advisory Council (elected by People of Color Caucus)
Youth Office program staff

Youth Council
(meets annually in August)

7 at-large adults
4 at-large youth
25 youth representatives
People of Color Caucus
outgoing Steering Committee

Youth Office

3 YRUU programs specialists
youth programs director
administrative assistant

UUA Administration

UUA Board of Trustees

Arrows/labels: selects · elects and directs · directs programs · directs · selects YPSs · implements decisions of · sponsors · advocates for youth · includes · oversees · elects for selecting the YRUU program specialists who work in the Youth Office.

Local YRUU groups take many shapes and forms across the continent. In some congregations, there is no differentiation between Sunday morning religious education and YRUU events. In others, the two structures are totally separate, one meeting Sunday mornings and the other Sunday evenings. Some youth attend only one of the meetings; others are involved in both.

Some congregations have only traditional religious education for their youth with "teachers" who use a formal curriculum. Some youth programs are overseen and supported by the congregation's Religious Education Committee; others are run by a committee made up of youth and adults. There is no one right program. Each congregation must develop a program that meets the needs of its youth.

Ideally the YRUU group has several adult advisors who meet with them regularly and with whom the youth can develop an intimate relationship that is neither parental nor academic.

Or, your group may not have regular advisors but may commandeer different adults for each event, particularly if the group meets on an informal basis. Sometimes a new group will start out with this level of commitment, evolving into a group that meets more regularly and with more consistent youth and adult leadership as members come to know and trust one another.

Conferences

Most districts have a youth and adult governing body, generally called a Youth/Adult Committee (YAC) or a District Youth Steering Committee. This is a committee or council that helps to coordinate and represent YRUU throughout the district. This committee is often responsible for putting on conferences within the district, developing district policies and bylaws, sponsoring training, reaching out to help congregations that want to start a youth group, maintaining a database of youth and advisors in the district, and publishing a newsletter. Refer to the handbook *From*

YACs to SACs: A Guide to District Youth Programming for more information about YACs.

District Conferences

At a district conference, youth from several congregations come together at one location for a few days, typically over a weekend. The conference usually includes workshops, worship, a dance, a talent show, and other events.

In some UUA districts, conferences are sponsored and coordinated by the district Youth/Adult Committee. In others, individual churches sponsor and host a conference for the whole district. Good places to get ideas and support for organizing a conference can be found in *How to Be a Con Artist: Youth Conference Planning Handbook for Unitarian Universalists, From YACs to SACs: A Guide to District Youth Programming,* and other resources listed in "For More Information" at the end of this handbook.

The Youth Social Justice Conference

This conference started as a joint effort of the UUA's Washington Office and the Youth Office to train youth in the skills to create social change. Originally held in Washington, D.C., this annual conference focused on the impact of citizen advocacy on national government. The conference now meets in a different location every year and concentrates on giving youth the skills to plan and participate in grassroots community campaigns that can effect change within YRUU, their congregations, and their communities. Contact the Youth Office for more information.

Anti-racism and the Journey Toward Wholeness

With the goal of world community and justice for all people, YRUU has become a powerful force for anti-racist transformation of Unitarian Universalism, and seeks to influence the the larger society as well. Following the 1999 Youth Council Resolution, "It's Time We Did Something About Racism in YRUU!" in which YRUU committed to work actively to dismantle systemic oppression,

YRUU has initiated several changes to further this goal.

YRUU now works to incorporate caucusing and discussion around issues of race and identity into its conferences. These discussions are known as *identity groups, identity caucuses,* or *raps* and generally involve both white youth and youth of color. The groups hold simultaneous but separate discussions, usually facilitated by a youth with anti-racism training who identifies with the designation of the group. The groups operate on the principle that our communities will be affirming of people of all identities when each of us is aware of our own identity and how power and privilege affect us individually. These identity groups help us in our process of identity formation, letting us explore in a safe atmosphere the way in which racism and other forms of oppression have affected both those who have been oppressed and those who have experienced privilege due to their identity. This is important because we live in a society that denies and minimizes the effect of racism and other oppressions in our lives. Youth in particular are often unaware of how deeply they have been affected. Weekend or week-long anti-racism conferences are another important part of YRUU's anti-oppression work. These anti-racism conferences involve a youth-led model of the UUA's Jubilee World workshop, which works to dispel common misunderstandings Unitarian Universalists have regarding racism and focuses on personal reflection as well as the transformation of institutions and the larger culture in which they operate. Facilitators for workshops on the local, district, or continental level are available through the Youth Office.

The Role of an Advisor

Advising youth can take many different forms. You could be part of a team of advisors that meets weekly with a local youth group. Or you might meet occasionally with the youth group as a support person for the group's advisors, as a driver on field trips, or as an extra adult for overnights and other activities. Some youth advisors teach a religious education course on Sunday mornings. Some work with junior high school youth, while others work with only high school youth. You might be a mentor in a youth group's coming-of-age program. Or you might be an advisor on the district Youth/Adult Committee or an advisor who attends district conferences.

You may decide that working directly with youth is not the best role for you, but you can still show your support for youth programming by advocating for youth within your congregation. You can contribute to the group's fundraising efforts, drive a youth committee member to meetings, flip pancakes at an overnight breakfast, or speak out in support of youth issues at your church's annual meeting.

There is no one path in youth advising. Many people first work with a local youth group, then find themselves volunteering for district programming, and later become involved continentally. Vary your experience to find the place that suits you best and to keep yourself from burning out.

Advising in a Local Youth Group

Advisors who work in local youth groups can have a wide variety of experiences. They might work with anywhere from two to more than twenty youth, with junior youth groups or senior youth groups, alone or as part an advising team of two to even five or six. Local youth group advisors might be supervised by the director of religious education, minister, Youth/Adult Committee, professional youth coordinator, or a combination of the above.

Advisors to a new youth group or a younger group of kids may find themselves leading most of the programming themselves. If the group has been around for a while and has developed strong leadership skills, then the advisor will mostly need to support the youth leadership that is already in place.

Advising at Conferences

Some advisors attend district conferences or continental events, while others focus on local youth group overnights and excursions. Advisors can find themselves volunteering anywhere from two to ten hours a week for their youth group work. Some will be reimbursed for their expenses or given an honorarium or salary, while others will not. (Serving as an advisor should never result in any personal costs.)

Advisors who volunteer for district conferences will be involved with youth in a very different setting than those who do local youth group advising only. They will be making a two- or three-day, sometimes even a week-long, commitment to attend a conference with programming designed for youth. They may be asked to drive youth to and from the conference or to lead a workshop once they are there. But unless you are one of the adults on the staff or planning committee for the conference, you will have fewer responsibilities at a conference than you do at your local events. Adults who are not on staff for the event are just conferees; they don't have to run things. They are there to offer advice and support if requested and to respond in emergencies, but generally they are there to have fun.

Your sleeping arrangements and food will probably be quite different from what you are used to when you travel. You may find yourself sleeping on hard church floors or lumpy camp mattresses and eating vegan food. But conferences allow an advisor to establish deeper rapport with youth. The conference experience is often more intense than weekly meetings. You will also have the chance to connect and share resources with adults from other congregations who are also involved in youth work.

All over the country, districts have trouble getting enough qualified, competent, caring adults to serve as conference advisors. Although, like all other aspects of advising it varies by district, the role of the conference advisor is primarily one of modeling. An advisor goes to a conference to interact with youth, to be an adult who is not in a parental or authoritarian role, and to give youth a chance to relate to adults on a more equal footing. For many adults, this can be a rewarding and rejuvenating experience.

There should be an orientation meeting for adults at the start of each conference. If it is at your congregation, ask the youth on the conference staff to make sure that the new advisors are welcomed and included. And make sure that advisors are put in "touch groups." Touch groups are small groups of six to ten participants who "touch base" with each other periodically through the conference by playing games or engaging in other activities to help the group bond.

One of the biggest challenges for an advisor new to conferences is connecting with the youth. It often helps to bring some activity that people can easily join in: Start playing your guitar, kicking a hacky sack, or throwing a Frisbee, and soon you will quickly be surrounded by youth. Or bring a bag with crayons, markers, and coloring books. Find a table, spread everything out, and start coloring. Other artists will soon join you. Your particular interests or hobbies can be a path to meeting and making friends with youth.

Advising for a Larger Community

Adults who advise for district youth/adult committees or other district youth governing bodies may find themselves attending monthly committee meetings and attending district conferences. These adults will be working with some of the most active and motivated youth leadership. They will often be asked to help other advisors in the district with ideas for youth programming and to function as a youth advocate in the district. Other responsibilities include serving as liaisons between youth and the district board of trustees, the religious education committee, the local UU Ministers' Association chapter, people-of-color organizations, or other concerned adults.

Some adults also choose to work with youth on the continental level by serving as an at-large delegate at Youth Council. These adults share their local and district youth group experiences with youth and adults from all over the United States and Canada, and have the opportunity to establish closer relationships with some of the most experienced youth leaders from across the continent.

Qualities of a Good Advisor

According to a policy established by the YRUU Youth Council, advisors need to be at least twenty-five to participate in Youth Council. Districts and congregations can set their own age requirements or follow this continental guideline.

Whether an advisor is twenty-five or forty-five, age is less important than how comfortable an advisor is as an *adult*. Advisors must be comfortable with exercising authority and leadership within a youth group when it is called for, but they should not need authority and leadership roles to enhance their own self-image.

Nor should advisors feel that they have to mirror the values and behaviors of youth in order to be liked. The integrity with which an advisor articulates and acts upon his or her own belief system is much more important. Advisors are models, not mirrors. The last thing a young person wants to see in an advisor is a reflection of her/himself.

A good advisor must also be aware of his or her own gender, racial/ethnic, and sexual/affectional orientation identities. In particular, it's important to be aware of the power dynamics associated with that identity. Given the YRUU focus on anti-racism and anti-oppression, it is important that advisors receive training in these areas. Youth will be looking for mentors in this work and will need strong advisors to join them in exploring how oppression works in our youth groups, in our congregations, and in society at large. Contact the UUA Youth Office for more information about participating in anti-oppression training.

Advisors must maintain clear boundaries between themselves and youth. These include sexual and emotional boundaries. Advisors should never look to youth to meet their emotional or sexual needs. Romantic/sexual relationships between advisors and youth are damaging and unacceptable under any circumstances. Just as it is appropriate for youth to look to their peers in the youth group for support with personal issues, advisors should look to their own peers for this kind of personal support.

Who you are with youth is far more important than the specific tasks you perform. At a brainstorming session with youth and advisors at a Pacific Central District Conference, participants came up with the following desirable advisor characteristics. A good youth advisor

- is fun, helpful, eclectic, sensitive, nurturing, drug-free, vulnerable, accessible, courageous, responsible, comfortable, a good listener, honest, flexible, genuine, interesting, neither evasive nor invasive, and tolerant of noise and mess
- has a sense of humor, a great vision of Unitarian Universalism, facilitation skills, a strong sense of personal worth, an answering machine, and a solid sense of his or her sexual identity
- brings munchies
- leads with a participatory style
- sets personal limits
- works well with others
- provides transportation
- wants to be an advisor
- likes and respects kids as people

The same group brainstormed the following list of characteristics that don't work well in an advisor. A youth advisor should not

- be untrustworthy, uncommitted, a gossiper, condescending, undependable, needy, a couch potato, judgmental, opinionated, controlling, immature, a lecturer, without a vision, inflexible, negative, abusive, flaky, rude, or lazy
- have unresolved issues from his or her own adolescent years, a private agenda out of synch with UU values, boundary issues, or a parental attitude
- try to practice therapy on the group

Being a good youth advisor means being genuine with youth. This is frequently frightening for adults, who have developed effective personas for dealing with the world. In a youth group, youth are struggling to answer questions of how to be. They will challenge you to be vulnerable and real. You can help them see what it's like to be responsible, caring, and involved. You can show them by example what it means to be a Unitarian Universalist and to live out our values in day-to-day life. The youth you are advising are surrounded by adults who relate to them in the context of specific roles—parent, teacher, other authority figures. You are giving them an opportunity to know at least one adult just as a person. A youth group can go only as far as the leaders are willing to take it. Whatever your leadership style, you will always have more power than any of the youth in the group. If you expect them to be open and honest during a meeting, you will need to create a space for that to happen. You can do that by being open and honest yourself. Being who you are can give the youth permission to be who they are. Let them see how you handle mistakes, how you deal with your feelings, how you handle conflict. At the same time, you need to remember that there are always boundaries between you and the youth. You are not there to work on your own personal issues. You want to be genuine and real with the youth, but always remember that they are not there to support you emotionally. Imagine that you have had one of those "weeks from hell." You come to the YRUU meeting feeling frustrated and irritable. It won't work for you to pretend to be cheerful—the youth will see right through your act.

What will work is for you to be honest about how you are without asking the youth to either fix your feelings or join you in them. During check-in time you could say something like: "I have had a really frustrating week and I'm feeling irritable, but I am ready to be here and hope to have a good meeting with the group." Enough said. You have been honest, vulnerable, and clear without asking the youth to provide you with an emotional bridge.

Empowering Youth

As a youth group advisor, one of your key responsibilities is to promote youth empowerment. If you do your job correctly, you will find that you are not in control of the group and will not be able to determine outcomes through direct action. This poses a dilemma, however, since parents and other adults in the congregation regard you as ultimately responsible for the group's actions—especially when things go badly. This responsibility without control leads inevitably to a kind of anxiety that can be calmed only if you are confident that even if everything goes wrong, everything will ultimately be okay.

How do you get to this ideal state? By training other adult advisors and youth leaders well. If you actively create a team environment of trust and accountability, you will build an atmosphere in which bad things happen less often and less severely, as well as a process in which the youth group members and their adult advisors can handle problems themselves. In this type of program, youth are empowered and feel free to act creatively—even whimsically—without making adults in the congregation excessively nervous.

Because this ideal state is hard to achieve and maintain, a youth group advisor must constantly reassess the balance between leading and advising. A youth group that has not yet learned to steer itself may need an advisor who is a more active leader. A group that has achieved what its members regard as the ideal state may feel squashed or disempowered if the advisor fails to recognize this and continues to lead too much.

Finally, a group that has achieved the ideal balance will lose it if it fails to pass along what it has learned to the next generation of youth and adult leaders. In youth group terms, a generation is every two to four years, and values and norms change with each successive generation. This constant turnover makes the youth group advisor's job tricky, since an advisor's role may well need to change from year to year.

Youth need to own their decisions and their consequences. They are full of energy, enthusiasm, and vision, but sometimes they don't know how to turn their ideas from vision into reality. That's where you come in. If a group has never planned an overnight event, they may not know what tasks need to be accomplished to pull it off. See if you can give this advice in a way that allows them to take responsibility for the tasks themselves, which will teach them much more than if they only watch you do the work. And when youth complete a job successfully, they feel good about themselves and what they have accomplished.

Moreover, adults who try to do it all themselves tend to burn out quickly. If you let go of the reins a little, you'll see how things can be different yet still work well. When the youth do most of the leading, you will be amazed at how creatively and competently they can pull it off.

Sometimes youth may fail and you will have to rush in and pick up the pieces. At other times, when they don't follow through with their responsibilities, it may be more appropriate to let a project fail so that they can learn from their mistakes.

Advisors must tread a fine line between rescuing the group all the time and letting members learn to live with the consequences of their actions. Experience is the best teacher of where that line is, but safety is the most important consideration. If anybody is in any danger, by all means, step in and straighten things out. You can always call a meeting once everyone is safe and ask the group members to take responsibility for what happened and come up with a response.

Even if your leadership style is very collaborative, you are always a role model. Your tone and level of commitment will in many ways determine the group's complexion or attitude. It is important that you set a tone of interest and enthusiasm so the participants will be interested and enthusiastic, too. If you are nonchalant, they will be as well. Groups whose advisors have a positive, "can do" attitude get lots more accomplished.

There are a variety of resources available to you as an advisor to assist with leadership development in your group. Contact your district Youth/Adult Committee regarding training in your area. If a district asks, the UUA Youth Office will send a pair of trainers, one youth and one adult, to facilitate a Leadership Development Conference, an Advisor Training, or a Spirituality Development Conference. Additional resources are listed on page 59 of this handbook.

Parents as Advisors

Parents of teenage youth make some of the best advisors. They are among the most motivated adults, since they have a strong interest in making sure their kids have a wonderful youth group experience. Whenever parents serve as advisors, though, it is important for them to get their teenagers' permission.

Sometimes children who didn't mind having their parents as advisors when they were young find the situation increasingly uncomfortable as they grow older. It can be difficult to open up and really be themselves with Mom or Dad there. When this happens, the parent, not the youth, needs to leave the group. A teen's youth group experience should never be sacrificed for the advising experience of the parent.

If you have YRUU-age children, please discuss the issue with them at length before you take on youth group advising. And check in with them periodically to make sure that it is still okay with them for you to be there.

The Advisor as Go-Between

Try as you may to encourage the adults in your religious community to interact directly with the youth, many adults just aren't used to relating directly to younger people. You may find yourself serving as a liaison between the two age groups, but you can be instrumental in breaking down the barriers between the generations.

Suppose, for example, that someone from your church's Social Action Committee calls you to see if the YRUU group would be interested in participating in a campaign to feed the homeless. You could ask the group and then relay their reaction back to the social action chairperson, or you could suggest that the chairperson speak directly to a youth in your group whom you know to be very interested in social action. Better yet, you could ask the chairperson to come to the youth group meeting and talk with the entire group about the campaign.

In your role as a youth group advisor, you may also find yourself becoming a youth advocate. When conflicts arise between youth and adults, you may be put in the middle. Your situation is often a sticky one: trying to educate adults to deal with youth as responsible individuals, while at the same time trying to educate youth on how to be responsible.

Because adults are in a more powerful position than youth in our society, it is extremely difficult for a youth to disagree with or contradict an adult. Even if you agree with the other adults that the youth have made a mistake, it is important that you try to advocate for them. They need an adult who can present the situation from their perspective while helping them to rectify the situation. Yours may be the only voice expressing their point of view.

For example, suppose your youth group requested the use of the church for an overnight. They received permission from all of the appropriate authorities, but the director of religious education gave them specific instructions not to use any of the supplies in the arts-and-crafts cabinet. You then find out the following Sunday that the director of religious education has banned all future youth overnights at the church because the construction paper, crayons, and glue were used.

While talking to the youth, you learn that Rachel, who had been absent the day that the instructions were given, used the supplies because she didn't know they were off limits. You recognize that the youth are still responsible for having used the supplies and that someone should have oriented Rachel to the rules.

The youth group comes up with a proposal to rectify the situation. They will raise funds to replace the supplies by holding a bake sale after church. They also promise that from now on they will orient all participants at the start of all overnights. You and the youth make the proposal to the director of religious education, and even though she is reluctant to trust the youth again, you do your best to present the youths' perspective.

Networking

It's hard to be an effective advisor alone. Whenever possible, try to advise in a team. It not only provides variety, balance, and an opportunity for time off, but it also means you won't have to bear the entire responsibility for advising alone.

The youth also benefit from having more than one advisor. They see you modeling cooperation and sometimes conflict resolution. They also have the opportunity to connect with more than one adult, so that one adult does not have to try to be everything to every youth.

You can also get support from advisors outside your congregation. Start an advisor network in your district. You can publish an occasional newsletter to share ideas, hold quarterly get-togethers, and/or host an annual district advisor training (contact the UUA Youth Office for more information). If you want to meet other advisors, attend a district conference. It is rewarding and energizing to connect with others who share your enthusiasm for and commitment to working with youth.

YRUU Youth

YRUU is continually challenged to meet the needs of the current generation of youth. Young people coming of age today are living in a very different world from the one most advisors inhabited during their adolescence. But whether you are advising on a local, district, or continental level, the youth around you are facing similar issues. They are going through tremendous changes, both physically and emotionally. Their ability to reason and comprehend abstract thought is developing in new ways, and the world around them is presenting ever increasing challenges.

Youth experience tremendous developmental changes—physically, emotionally, intellectually, spiritually, and socially—between the ages of twelve and twenty. Younger teens are focused both on determining their own identity and their place within the groups to which they belong: Who am I in the world? Where do I belong? Which groups am I a member of? Who is the "us" and what do we believe? Who is the "them" and what do they believe? How do I behave to make sure I belong?

As youth reach their mid- and later-teens, they become more focused on individuation—more critical of the groups to which they belong—and look for ways in which they agree or disagree with the values and definitions of those groups: Do I really agree with what my family has always taught me about politics? Do I think my church's stance on reproductive rights is correct? Is what my friends do really cool? What were once clear distinctions between "us" and "them" become fuzzier as youth grow increasingly concerned with carving out their own place and distinguishing themselves from others.

Youth also develop empathy for others as they learn to look at a situation from a variety of viewpoints. When they were younger they determined their behavior by how well it would be accepted by a group. Now they consider what is fair, just, and right. They begin to look outward to issues of community, politics, privilege, oppression, and social action.

Teens often say they don't feel as if they fit in. They describe themselves as wearing a mask or just playing a part; they are not able to simply be themselves. Even if outwardly it appears that they fit in and are accepted by their peer group, internally they may not be quite sure that they really belong. Acceptance is a frequent issue for all of us throughout our lives, but learning to feel okay just the way they are is crucial for young people's self-esteem. As a part of that acceptance, youth want to be recognized for their skills and special gifts; they want to be treated with respect and to be trusted.

Youth develop at different paces and in a variety of ways. The youngest member of your youth group may be the most mature. The most physically developed may act like the youngest kid. And don't be surprised when they change from one day to the next—the president of the youth group may have acted "together" and responsible when reporting to the board and then behaved like a silly goof-off the next day at an overnight.

Make no assumptions about youth by how they present themselves to you. The shy, quiet youth may be waiting for someone to offer an opportunity to lead. The boisterous youth with lots of bravado may be faking, hoping for acceptance. Even though you may be working with only one age group, that can be vastly diverse.

As they strive to grow and learn about themselves and the world, youth seek opportunities to spread their wings. They need to taste adulthood and try it out. They want to prove their competence. Most of us remember adolescence as a time of struggle and discovery. Although what was happening in the world around us may have been a bit different when we were young, today's youth must choose their path as we chose ours. Youth today may confront issues at a younger age than we did, but essentially they are on the same journey that we took.

Outside Issues and Pressures

As if figuring out who they are, what they believe, and where they fit in were not enough to deal with, our North American culture presents youth with many other issues and pressures: pressure from parents and school to succeed, and peer pressure on a variety of issues they will have to make choices about, such as drugs, sex, politics, AIDS, smoking, gangs, and violence. Although we also dealt with most of these issues during our teen years, the level of exposure and intensity is stronger today. Youth are constantly bombarded with media images of violence and exploitation. Violent crime and the number of violent deaths have increased, and the media never fail to make sure that these incidents are always at the top of our consciousness. The presence of AIDS and other sexually transmitted diseases has changed the way we address sex and relationships, forcing our young people to face the possibility of their own mortality at a much younger age than previous generations.

Youth look to YRUU and their peers in their congregations to help them face these issues and to make choices. YRUU can provide a safe place to discuss and explore difficult topics openly. If an intelligent decision is an informed decision, youth need avenues for open discussion, exploration, and support.

Identity Development

Identity is one of the most basic and yet most complex dimensions of human development. Whether they are conscious of it or not, youth face a variety of identity issues. Some of these will be based on choice while others (and this often comes as a surprise) may begin to emerge in a fluid experiential setting.

In a society like the United States, where rugged individualism is deeply rooted in the foundational identity of the nation, it is easy to believe that individuals determine their own identities. It is especially easy for youth to believe that they are in charge of their own identities and their own decisions. We do, indeed, have a primary role in shaping who we are. At the same time, we form our identities in relation to one another. In other words, identity is largely a *social* phenomenon. Part of who we are is determined by what groups we belong to and participate in, whether actively or passively. We hold both a personal identity and a social identity simultaneously. The two are integrally related: Group membership is not simply tacked on to a person, but is a "real, true, and vital part" of how we function in relation to identity groups. Individuals are shaped by social and environmental factors and by the culture in which they co-exist.

In addition to individual and group identity, institutions also have identities, which may or may not be consistent with individual or group identities. While Unitarian Universalism is a pluralistic religion, there is also a dominant—and very particular—Unitarian Universalist cultural identity. In working with youth, it may be easy to identify those youth who appear to stand out in the group for their *lack* of interest or participation. As a facilitator, you may wish to explore (on your own or with the youth) the identity characteristics of Unitarian Universalism. You can then pay attention to which youth fit seamlessly into Unitarian Universalist institutional and cultural identity, and which ones seem to exist in contrast to the dominant institutional culture. What are the implications for the youth group and how well it includes, welcomes, and supports all youth in the religious community? Identity is too important an issue for advisors to ignore. Take advantage of opportunities to learn more through reading and workshops.

A Welcoming Youth Group

A YRUU youth group is the perfect environment for encouraging youth to live out their Unitarian Universalist values by creating a just, compassionate, and affirming environment. This means creating a safe community that welcomes gay, lesbian, bisexual, and transgender youth; youth from gay or lesbian families; youth of color; multiracial youth; youth from multiracial families; youth with different physical abilities; and youth from various socioeconomic classes.

Many of the youth in your group are exploring their sexual identity. For lesbian, gay, bisexual, or transgender youth, YRUU may be the only safe haven where they can be themselves and still be accepted. If you always refer to people assuming that everyone is heterosexual, you will inadvertently convey that bias in what you say, asking girls if they have a boyfriend and boys if they have a girlfriend, for example.

These assumptions reinforce society's stereotypes of heterosexuality as the only acceptable sexuality. Always assume that there is at least one lesbian, gay, bisexual, or transgender youth, or one from a gay or lesbian family, in your group at all times. There probably is.

Our society does not offer gay, lesbian, bisexual, and transgender youth healthy images or role models. Bring in films or books that are gay-positive and share them with your youth group.

Have discussions that focus on sexuality issues and challenge any stereotypes or put-downs. Lead the UUA curriculum *Beyond Pink and Blue* or *Our Whole Lives,* available from the UUA Bookstore. Offer your gay, lesbian, bisexual, and transgender youth adult UU role models with whom they can identify. Invite these adults to speak to your group or serve as an advisor for conferences.

Our youth groups are primarily "white of European descent," but they are increasingly more ethnically diverse than the adult population in our congregations. Youth of color in your group may be part of a family with two parents of color, one parent of color, or no parent of color. They may have one or two parents in the home. They may or may not be adopted. If adopted, their parents may or may not be white and may be heterosexual or gay or lesbian. Youth of color and their families may be lifelong UUs or newcomers to our faith community.

In our congregations, there are four main constituencies of youth of color: youth whose biological parents are both people of color and whose family attends a UU congregation; adopted youth of color (primarily by white parents) whose families attend UU congregations; multiracial youth of color who are lifelong Unitarian Universalists (generally with an active white parent in the congregation); and multiracial youth of color who are new to Unitarian Universalism. These distinctions are meant to help youth leaders understand the dynamics at play, and to recognize that the experience of youth of color—while different from that of white youth—is itself diverse. Anecdotal evidence has shown that during the 1990s, youth of color tended to leave youth programs and UU congregations earlier than their white youth counterparts. This may be due in part to the identity development of youth of color and the lack of mentors of color, a community of color, and anti-racism analysis within reasonable reach of youth leaders. UU organizations such as Diverse and Revolutionary Unitarian Universalist Multicultural Ministries (DRUUMM) may be of help; they are committed to strengthening Unitarian Universalism's institutional ability to support and empower people of color in UU congregations and organizations.

One way youth leaders can support youth of color is to welcome and encourage questions related to racial and cultural identity. For many youth of color, including those who are adopted, racial/ethnic/cultural questions often come up years before they do for white youth. These questions are linked to their delicate burgeoning self-awareness, identity exploration, struggle against internalized racism and assimilation, and attempts to reclaim cultural identity and an individual sense of power. Youth need to be empowered and supported in these feelings, and encouraged to keep up their struggles. Adult advisors of youth groups including youth of color are strongly encouraged to network with DRUUMM and the wider church to help strengthen relationships between youth of color and Unitarian Universalism. Youth group leaders may also want to invite guest speakers from the community or congregation each year to intentionally address the issues of race and racism. A conversation about racism in schools, for example, would be of interest to youth. You might make these forums an annual tradition.

Also consider activities such as field trips to local ethnic restaurants, cultural heritage sites, and museums, combined with follow-up conversations about the experience. As you make connections with local people of color and allies, you may find they are valuable resources to lead workshops at youth conferences. Youth exchanges with other denominations, such as African-American Baptist, Korean Presbyterian, African Methodist Episcopal, or other multiracial churches can be positive. The UUA curriculum *Neighboring Faiths* may be helpful in designing an experience with another faith community.

But be aware of power and privilege in developing these connections. Seek authentic relationships through long-term planning rather than short-term feel-good activities that may be token efforts. Look for ways to address the underlying issues of racism. Involving UU adults of color is a great way to facilitate these kinds of exchanges, or consider working with DRUUMM.

One youth group in Chicago developed an outreach program with youth of color from the area, opening up their group to youth from nearby shelters and group homes. They challenged adult members of their congregation to provide transportation to and from church, offer scholarships for youth to attend conferences, and become "big sisters, brothers, and grandparents" of youth who came to the church. YRUU groups can help congregations "walk their talk" around issues of racial justice.

Increasing numbers of useful resources are available from the UUA or your District Office or YAC. These include *Race to Justice, Creating a Jubilee World, Racial & Cultural Diversity Task Force Report, Youth-Focus Anti-Racism Training,* and *DRUUMM Youth of Color/White Allies Conferences and Trainings.*

The growing number of young people of color in our faith community continues to challenge us all to address issues of race, racism, cultural appropriation, and cultural identity. Your awareness of these issues is critical to helping our UU institutions create the systems and programs necessary to provide consistent and effective support for people of color.

Unitarian Universalist youth with disabilities can also find a welcoming environment in YRUU. Youth who are segregated in "special" classes at school and labeled as "different" by their peers can attend a YRUU youth group and be accepted for who they are. Make sure that any activities the group plans are inclusive of all members of the group. If the group wants to do a spiral dance for their worship, for example, ask them how they can arrange it so that the participant who walks with crutches can participate.

Don't make the youth with a disability take all the responsibility for advocating for his/her needs. Make inclusivity a goal for the entire youth group so everyone is working for it at all times.

Youth and the Congregation

Youth are blessed with a great deal of energy and the motivation to learn, create, and make an impact on their world. Congregations can benefit from the enthusiasm and passion that they bring to worship, social action, community outreach, and other areas of congregational life. Youth can serve on congregational governing bodies, be on a planning committee for the church retreat, lead religious education classes, be part of a Sunday service, and participate in the all-church cleanup.

Youth want to be welcomed. They want to feel that they are part of their congregational community, just as adults do. If the only time adults invite youth to be involved in church programming is to do the dishes after the alliance lunch or babysit during the all-church potluck, the congregation is sending the youth a message that they aren't valued much except for their clean-up skills or babysitting prowess. If that is the only message the youth hear, they may well not want to stick around.

Youth should be an integral part of all church programming. They should be included in worship services, have direct representation within the church governing bodies, and participate in church fundraising events. Congregations that view youth as whole individuals and valuable members of their communities will help them develop into mature, self-confident Unitarian Universalist adults, while enriching the entire congregation.

Many congregations sponsor coming-of-age programs for their youth. These programs help youth focus with their peers and adult mentors on some of the issues and concerns they have about growing up as Unitarian Universalists in today's world. These programs often culminate with a Sunday service that recognizes their achievements and celebrates their joining the congregation. Most congregations develop their own programs, but you can contact the UUA Youth Office for a list of ideas and resources.

The age at which congregations permit a person to join and sign the membership book varies from congregation to congregation. Check with your society's bylaws to see what the age is for your congregation. When one signs the membership book, there is often a meeting with the minister, recognition at a Sunday service, a potluck with the membership committee, and/or a visit by a canvasser. Make sure that youth are not slighted in any of these rituals of membership.

Even though some youth may have been around the congregation since they were very young, their decision to join is no less monumental than that of the adults who are joining. In many ways it is more momentous, since this may be one of a youth's first decisions to become a member of something as an independent young adult. (It is, we hope, not a decision that has been defined for them by their parents, school, or peer group.)

Many Unitarian Universalist churches balk at permitting youth to join the congregation. As a member congregation of the UUA, each church is requested to pay the UUA a specific annual amount for each member to support the Annual Program Fund. This money goes toward the operating costs of the Association and services to our congregations and districts. Because youth have little or no income and are frequently unable to pledge, many churches feel they cannot afford to have youth members. It is good to question a congregation's values when membership guidelines are developed. Ask which is more important: the youth, or the few dollars it would cost to recognize youth as a valued part of the congregation.

Some states have laws that no one under age eighteen may vote on issues involving money. Several congregations have developed "associate" member programs that allow youth to belong and participate as every other member does, except that they are not allowed to vote on financial matters.

Let's remind our adult members that the youth within our congregations are part of our community. They may not meet on Sunday morning. They may be less visible than the younger kids or older members, but they are still an integral part of who we are as a religious community, and their contributions enrich us. Youth are also tomorrow's adult members. If we do not provide a place for them in our churches, they are less likely to remain Unitarian Universalists as adults.

Non-Unitarian Universalist Youth

Many local youth groups ask whether youth who are not Unitarian Universalists can attend and become members. These youth often come as friends of UU youth group members, who want to share what they have found here with others whom they care about. If we don't reject adults who visit to see if Unitarian Universalism is something that fits with their values, then we shouldn't reject youth either. Please welcome and encourage all youth, Unitarian Universalist or not, who attend your meetings.

Youth ministry is about helping youth to become loving, caring, and competent adults. Many adults in our congregations came to Unitarian Universalism from other religious backgrounds. Some joined our denomination after their involvement in YRUU, or Liberal Religious Youth before it. Some parents join our denomination as a result of their children's involvement in YRUU. The values that youth learn in YRUU are clear; youth who do not share these values tend to go elsewhere.

Youth as Unitarian Universalists

Most YRUU youth identify themselves as Unitarian Universalists. They may not go to church regularly, especially if there is little or no programming for them there, yet they do see themselves as Unitarian Universalists or they would not attend youth groups or conferences. YRUU groups across the continent vary as much as Unitarian Universalist congregations do, but there are several UU values consistent among all of them:

- Be respectful.
- Be concerned about each others' welfare.
- Be fair and non-judgmental.
- Do not practice put-downs or demeaning teasing.
- Make sure that everyone is heard.
- Be inclusive.
- Be genuine.

No youth group is mandated to subscribe to a particular set of values. Each group is encouraged to discover what it cherishes. The YRUU Youth Council developed the following mission statement for the continental organization of YRUU:

Young Religious Unitarian Universalists shall serve its members for the purposes of fostering spiritual depth, creating a peaceful community on earth and peace within us, and clarifying both individual and universal religious values as part of our growth process. Our purposes are to provide and manifest a greater understanding of Unitarian Universalism, and to encourage the flow of communication between youth and adults.

In so doing we shall nurture the freedom and integrity of the questioning mind, and embrace all persons of diverse backgrounds. We shall encourage the development of a spirit of independence and responsibility.

We shall strive to support our members and member groups with educational resources, a communications network, and with love.

These purposes shall assist us in developing an effective system for social action and serve to raise our levels of mutual respect, communication, and community consciousness.

In addition to considering themselves to be Unitarian Universalists and fostering Unitarian Universalist values, YRUU youth have contributed greatly to the denomination as a whole. The youth movements of the Universalists and Unitarians joined together before the adult denominations did. They merged in 1953, creating Liberal Religious Youth, preceding the consolidation of the American Unitarian Association and the Universalist Church of America by eight years.

Youth Group Nuts and Bolts

You can do many things to get a youth group up and running smoothly. The first steps to developing a strong youth group are understanding the specific needs of your group and creating an environment that will help you to address those needs. The level of direction you will have to provide will vary depending on the age of the participants. Junior high youth will have little experience in carrying forth their plans They often don't even know what questions to ask about how to plan an overnight or coordinate a social action event. They will depend on you to provide direction and guidance. With older, more experienced youth, your role will be more that of an advisor to their leadership.

When you arrive at a meeting, it's always a good idea to remain flexible and open to change. The meeting may go as the youth have planned; however, frequently things happen differently. The person who was supposed to coordinate the meeting might be overwhelmed by the project or have other difficulties. You can refocus any confusion and disappointment by having or creating an alternate plan, perhaps in keeping with the same theme.

For example, suppose the group was planning to make plaster masks. Because there was confusion about who was supposed to buy the bandages, you don't have materials to make plaster masks.

Some possible alternatives might be to make masks from paper plates or paper bags. Maybe you can discuss masks, both real and psychological. Maybe masks could be made out of less traditional materials. What you don't want to do is focus on someone's failure. You want to use this opportunity to allow the group's creativity to solve the problem. But in case no one has any ideas, always come prepared with a "grab bag" of alternative activities.

Sometimes more important events change your plans. As an advisor you need to stay alert for changes that may be more valuable or important to the group than the planned activity. Perhaps someone raised an important issue or personal crisis during check-in. A discussion of the issue while it is fresh in everyone's mind may be of greater value to the group than the planned activity. Making masks can wait until next week. Regardless of the age mix in your local group, be flexible and open to change.

Building Intimacy

New youth groups need to build intimacy and trust in order to work together, support one another in being themselves, have confidence in each other, and feel like a community. They can then focus their energy on the actions they want to accomplish.

Even if your local youth group has been meeting for several years, it will feel like a new group when you start with them. It will also be a new group after a summer hiatus, or when new youth join in the middle of the year. Whenever you are involved in a group of any kind, taking steps to help develop intimacy and build trust will significantly improve the group's interaction.

One model for how to build intimacy in youth groups was developed by Denny Rydberg. He talks about the five stages that a youth group must go through in order to take action as a group: bonding, opening up, affirming, stretching, and deeper sharing. The following material is adapted from his book *Building Community in Youth Groups*, published by Group Publishing, Inc.

Bonding

Bonding is the first stage in building community in a youth group. If individuals don't know who else is in the group, what they have in common, and how they are different, they will never feel comfortable enough to share, be supportive, and take action.

To bond, youth need to get to know each other. They need to start with emotionally low-risk activities that do not require them to reveal more about themselves than they are comfortable sharing.

Games or tasks, such as a scavenger hunt or cooking a meal together, are good bonding activities because they provide a goal and detailed instructions so that new members know what to do even if they have never been to a youth group meeting before. They also allow the youth get to know each other in a non-threatening way. If a group is new and one of their first activities is making a piñata for the church fair, they can chat over papier-mâché about where they go to school and what movies they like.

Opening Up

This happens naturally as a group spends more time together, and superficial sharing about interests and hobbies deepens to discussions about hopes, fears, and dreams. You can facilitate this in your group by offering time for check-ins or leading games that require the youth to share a little more deeply about their personal concerns and opinions.

Affirming

As youth open up to each other, you will want to make sure that they always respond to one another in a positive way. As they start to share their personal ideas and feelings, hearing another group member say, "Oh, that's stupid!" will ensure that they will be unwilling to open up and share again.

Remind the group that it is fine to disagree, but that all are entitled to their own opinions, and that as Unitarian Universalists we respect and honor a diversity of ideas. This is an area where the advisor can model the ideal behavior. If you continually affirm and support the youth and their ideas and efforts, they will be more likely to do the same for each other.

Stretching

A youth group "stretches" when it needs to respond to a situation beyond what usually occurs in its members' daily lives. Opportunities for such stretching should occur after the group has bonded, opened up, and experienced affirming each other. This could be something planned, like participating in a ropes course or visiting a hospice for children with AIDS. But it can also be something unplanned, as when someone's parents get a divorce or someone is hospitalized after a car accident.

Youth groups that successfully face and respond to stretching moments tend to become very close as a group and work well together. Unfortunately, youth who are faced with a stretching experience before they are ready will often be scared away by the intimacy of the experience. Whenever possible, try to introduce stretching opportunities when the youth group is ready for it.

Deeper Sharing

Once group members have faced a challenge and successfully responded to it in a supportive way, they will be much more likely to open up and share even deeper thoughts and feelings. They will be willing to take risks together, knowing that the community will support them in whatever they face. This is when youth will be ready to share their fears about coming out as lesbian, gay, bisexual, or transgender; to cry about the betrayal they feel that a parent left them and has made no attempt to be in touch for years; or to celebrate the joy of a first love and relationship. A community that can share deeply with another in a supportive way is ready to take action.

If a new member joins a group that is already a tight community, then the group will have to back up to the first steps to bring the newcomer up to speed. If you are planning a deeper sharing activity and a new person is visiting, quickly have the group play a game or do a task together so the newcomer feels comfortable and connected enough to go on with the group. It will take a new person less time to bond with a tight community than it initially took the larger community to feel connected.

In addition to trusting one another, it is paramount that the group come to trust you as their advisor. This can happen only over time. There are many adults who deal with youth by saying one thing and doing another. Make sure you are very clear with your group about the kinds of matters you cannot keep confidential. (For more information on this topic, see "Creating a Safe Group.")

Once you have agreed on what is not confidential, everything else that is discussed in the group must be kept within the group—including some things that may not seem important to you. Even something as seemingly innocent as a comment to a parent that his or her son read a poem he wrote in worship may be construed by the youth as a breaking of trust. The youth may not want his parent to know that he writes poetry, or may not want to be asked to share it with his family. After you have been advising for a while and built trust with your youth group, it may be okay to discuss some things outside of the group, but you will have to develop a sense of that over time.

Confidential does not necessarily mean secret. As an advisor, you may feel you need to discuss problems from the youth group with someone else. Remember, you are not working in a vacuum.

You have religious professionals, the minister, and/or religious educator working with you in your youth ministry. Use your director or minister of religious education and/or parish minister as a resource for tough issues, but without disclosing the source, if possible.

See "Creating a Safe Group" for more information about when to break confidentiality. And don't forget that youth themselves can be a resource. The opportunity to discuss issues that are real and current is valuable for them and provides even more modeling for resolving those issues.

Covenants and Rules

Whenever a group is beginning to meet or has just gathered again after a hiatus, work on creating a covenant. A covenant is a set of rules or guidelines about how a group will interact together. Ask them: What are important qualities for making you feel safe in the group? How would you like to be treated as a member of this group?

Do this in a brainstorming session. Several elements consistent among youth covenants include the following: What is said in the group stays in the group; no put-downs or hurtful teasing; one person talks at a time; and members should be on time. Many covenants also call on participants to be present and attentive during hard conversations.

Sometimes a small group may be formed out of the larger youth group for a specific project, such as a committee to organize a social action event. Even when everyone already knows and has formed bonds with one another, it is still valuable to help the committee clarify how it wants to act as a group for this task. What are the specific ground rules for this group? Are there any special considerations?

You and your youth group may have to develop other rules and guidelines, such as rules for a conference at your church or for a trip to Boston. Behavior rules and consequences will vary according to the traditions, expectations, and norms of the families within the congregation. Struggles around issues of smoking and sleeping arrangements are common. Try to develop guidelines and rules that will lead to maximum safe participation in youth programs. Remember, the rules must be agreed to by at least four parties: the youth, the advisors, the YAC (or religious education committee if your congregation does not have a YAC), and the parents. Attention to these matters builds trust and safety. When youth and adults create and own the rules together, it lays the groundwork for mutual trust and respect.

The goal of rules is always the preservation of safety and community. Youth planning any event should establish rules well in advance and in accordance with these principles, in consultations with adult advisors, and with respect for the concerns of youth participants and their legal guardians and/or parents.

The following behavior guidelines were developed by the 1991 YRUU Youth Council as part of the Principles for the Establishment of Community. As you struggle to create rules and covenants for your group, you might wish to keep them in mind. They were developed primarily for the formation of conference rules, but they are relevant in forming rules under other circumstances.

- Ground rules and curfews should be based on knowledge of the area, rules of the host facility, and the age group participating.
- Rules in effect at any event should apply equally to all participants regardless of age.
- Rules should be developed in consideration of the needs of the youngest group attending.
- Sleeping arrangements should be provided to meet the needs of participants within the site conference (i.e., individuals' need for privacy and comfort, desires to share sleeping space with friends regardless of gender, and needs for quiet and peace).
- Participants should receive a behavior code with their registration packets and should be required to sign and return the form stating that they understand the rules and agree to abide by them.
- Rationales should always be provided with the rules.
- Conference rules should be read aloud to the entire group at the beginning of the conference

or event, with an opportunity for clarification by all parties.
- Participants under legal age should be required to provide a medical release form signed by a legal guardian and/or parent.
- All rules and guidelines should be made with consideration of state, provincial, and federal laws.
- Adults and older youth should be required to read, sign, and accept the "Code of Ethics for Adults and Older Youth."

Governing Styles

The governing style that your group chooses may evolve over time. As the members of the group grow up and move on, the group's needs will change.

Advisor Leading

With a new group or one composed primarily of younger members, you may want to start with an advisor leading most of the programming and grow into one of the other models as the group matures. But try to work yourself out of a leadership role as soon as possible. It's hard for youth to develop leadership skills if you continue to do everything, and advisor-directed groups tend to produce overworked, burned-out advisors. While you may initially spend more time supporting a group that is learning to lead itself than you would if you simply did things on your own, the amount of extra time you spend in the beginning will diminish as the youth learn how to lead themselves.

Group Leading

This method can be challenging for both the advisor and the group. With this model, there is no specific structure or procedure for who does what. Every project is undertaken by consensus, and leadership rotates. The problem is that if no one in the group "picks up the ball," the project will fall back on the advisor. A small group may do best with this style. If you have, for example, only one advisor and six youth, doing things by group consensus can be quite effective.

Elected Leadership

This is the traditional president–secretary–treasurer model—or, in youth group lingo, *facilitator, scribe,* and *money manager.* The drawbacks here are that quieter, more introverted youth may not be able to participate or compete. The elections process can also be divisive. But this style works in some groups. Traditional leadership roles can be educational and supportive to an active group.

Youth/Adult Committee (YAC)

This model works well with larger groups. The whole group chooses a smaller committee that is charged with carrying out the general plans agreed to by the group. YACs are usually made up of youth and adults in a three-to-one ratio. Facilitation of the committee is shared by its members, and decisions are generally made by consensus.

One of the advantages of using a YAC is that you can involve more of the congregation's adult leadership in youth programming. The committee may have a trustee, parent, or former advisor as a liaison with the congregation. The religious educator and advisors can serve on the committee *ex-officio.* This is one of the most successful models for active local groups, both in terms of leadership development and accomplishing goals.

Size Isn't Everything

The size of your group will fluctuate. Youth grow, change, and move on. You may have a very large group one year and a small group the next as many of the youth graduate and move away. The departure of an advisor or changes in the congregation may also affect your group's size.

Change of any kind will affect the group. Some people will like it and some people will vote with their feet. Although you want to provide positive ongoing YRUU meetings, don't be too concerned if the youth group isn't exactly the same as before. It is natural for groups to go through cycles, from large and active to smaller or even

nonexistent. Just don't give up. Continue to support the youth you have.

Sometimes you will have meetings attended by only a few people. It can be disconcerting if you plan for fifteen people and get three, but make sure you hold the meeting and make it valuable for the three people who do come. Focusing on those who don't show up will make the people who are present feel less worthy.

When There's Trouble

One of the toughest things about being a local youth group advisor is getting support for yourself. This is a primary reason to team up with other advisors. If you reach out to other adults in your church for support, they may become actively involved with the youth program. The more adults who interact with the youth, the more integrated the youth will become with the congregation as a whole. Have regular meetings with your religious education director and/or minister if possible. If your church has a YAC, make sure you attend its meetings.

And speaking of support, don't let your local youth group push you into cleaning up, taking minutes, or doing any other job that they don't want to do themselves. Make sure everyone helps with the hard tasks. As the advisor, you are still a member of the group. You need to make sure your rights are respected along with everyone else's.

Your youth group is a microcosm of the rest of the world—there will be the occasional crisis. Some problems will involve only a particular youth; others will affect the entire group. The support of your minister is valuable at such times. Sometimes youth groups will bring in a therapist or minister from the congregation to help deal with a particularly difficult situation, such as the death of a group member. Don't hesitate to call for help!

Your job is not to be a therapist but to be an adult advisor. Within that framework, you still want to care for and support the group and the individuals in it. In general, one of the best gifts you can give during a crisis is to make sure people have a place to talk about what's going on. When youth talk about tough or emotional issues, they often get nervous. They interrupt, they crack jokes, they try to divert the conversation away from the sensitive topic. You can help by encouraging them not to interrupt while others are talking and by bringing the focus back after a joke. This is a delicate balance. You don't want to push people to share if they don't want to. Monitor your own feelings about the crisis. Make sure that you get the emotional support you need outside of the group.

Disruptive Youth

Every youth group has at least one disruptive person—the youth who nixes everything, who interrupts or won't pitch in on any project, and who brings a lot of negative energy to the group—an advisor's worst nightmare. One of the best ways to deal with a disruptive youth is to figure out and respond to his or her motivation. It may be that the youth doesn't want to be in the group but is being forced to attend by a parent.

If that is the case, find out where the youth would rather be. She or he might be fascinated by toddlers and would like to help in the nursery. Maybe she or he wants to work with the sexton setting up coffee hour and fixing things around the church.

Some disruptive youth are just hungry for leadership opportunities they have never had. If you can channel their negative leadership in a positive direction, you will have a tremendous ally in the group. Don't forget to hold your youth accountable to the covenant they have made with each other, and ask them to be responsible for responding to any breaches in that covenant.

In one church, a junior high youth was so disruptive that he was told not to attend the youth group for the quarter. The minister asked him where in the church he would like to be involved on Sunday mornings. The boy thought that the church bookstore set up during coffee hour looked interesting, so he was made apprentice to the person who handled the bookstore. He never rejoined the youth group, but by the time he was in high school he was the head of the bookstore, doing all the accounting and book ordering.

Be careful not to pigeonhole youth. Your most disruptive youth one year may turn out to be your most dynamic leader the next. Youth grow and mature constantly, so give them the benefit of the doubt. You are most likely to get mature behavior from them if you always expect it.

Creating a Balanced Program

A balanced youth group program includes five components: community building, social action, worship, learning, and leadership development. This doesn't mean that the youth group needs to spend twenty percent of its time in each area.

As an advisor, you should encourage the youth to incorporate all these elements into their program, but be aware that they may need more of one or another at different times. For example, a new or younger youth group will need more community-building time until members feel bonded. Youth groups are generally not willing to worship together until they feel comfortable with each other. It is also important to realize that almost any activity has elements of more than one component.

Nothing can be accomplished until people know, trust, and care about each other and the group's success. Community building, or socializing, is time for people to get to know one another—time devoted to hanging out. Sometimes advisors tend to minimize the community-building or social component of youth groups. We tend to think that youth groups should always be educational and spiritual. Some of the most valuable experiences for youth happen during social activities. This is the time for them to bond together, share values, establish trust, generate intimacy, and practice acceptance. This is a special time—sometimes the only time—for Unitarian Universalist youth to share their liberal values. And the community they build here can help sustain and support them in their social interactions outside of YRUU. The rest of your congregation places an emphasis on the social element of their programs—imagine if there were no coffee hour, potluck dinners, fairs, or retreats. Make sure the youth have the same opportunities to socialize within their community. The YRUU group is one of the few unstructured places that youth have for getting together. School, religious education programs, and after-school sports or music lessons are all highly structured activities. Even when the youth group is involved with a more structured project, it is best to offer them some unstructured time, perhaps a half-hour gathering before or after the meeting. You can also try the following activities:

- *Game Night*
  Have group members bring board games or play physical games like tag or hide-and-seek. Games can generate sharing, as in the game in which everyone writes on a piece of paper something they think no one else knows about them. Someone then lists all the responses on a chalkboard or butcher paper, and people try to guess which item goes with which person. You

can learn surprising things about people with games like this.

- *Movie Night*
  Let the youth pick the movie, but be sure it has a rating appropriate for the group. Have youth bring sleeping bags. Maybe they can come to the meeting in their pajamas or dressed in theme outfits in keeping with the movie. Allow for time to talk about the movie; even comedies generate opinions. Don't forget the popcorn.
- *Parties*
  Theme parties are wonderful icebreakers for youth. They can really get into dressing up or creating unique menus.
- *Outings*
  Take your group on a beach trip, picnic, swimming pool, museum, or camping trip. But be sensitive to the economic situations of the individuals in the group; although ski trips and whitewater rafting can be wonderful, please be aware of youth who may not be able to participate in these events for financial reasons. You don't want anyone to feel excluded. If they want to, your group can raise the funds to make those more expensive events possible. Bake sales or car washes can be enjoyable community-building events, too.

Watch for power dynamics due to gender, race, class, ability, or sexual orientation. During social events, many of our youth feel that they cannot fully participate because their voices are drowned out by those in privileged positions. Youth advisors can monitor this situation and help people take part more fully.

Social Action

Because young people have passionate opinions about social issues, Unitarian Universalist youth have been at the forefront of social action initiatives. YRUU is a great place for youth to express and explore their values and put their concerns into action. As an advisor you can help them to channel these concerns into tangible results.

Let's say the group is interested in doing something to help the homeless. Your process may not be quite this formal, but the following list will give you an idea of the steps needed for a successful project.

1. *Select a project.*
   Identify a problem that generates high interest in the group and define it in a single sentence. For example, "Homelessness is a tragedy in our society, and we all have a responsibility to work to eradicate it."
2. *State your assumptions.*
   Briefly describe the social context in which the problem is found. Why is it a problem? Who suffers from it? How are they affected? What are the economic, political, and social factors involved? Is there something in our Unitarian Universalist Principles that can help us approach this problem? The group might spend time discussing how homelessness looks in their community. Are there laws that make it harder for the homeless to get back on their feet? Are there homeless youth as well as adults? What programs are already in place to help the homeless? This discussion will help the group to understand the overall issue and to narrow their focus in the next step.
3. *State the action plan.*
   Your planned action should be specific, measurable, achievable, and consistent with the group's values, such as making sandwiches and distributing them to the homeless at a park near the church.
4. *Develop a plan of accountability.*
   In working for justice we must reflect the changes we wish to see in the world in our own strategy and process. The most successful social action projects apply the same principles of empowerment and good communication between youth and adults that are the hallmark of effective youth programs. In order to make ourselves accountable to those whom our project will affect, we need to plan. Some questions to ask in developing a plan of accountability are: Who are our allies in this endeavor? Who in the community is already

engaged in this struggle? How can we offer our time, creativity, and other resources to them? Whom should we involve in our planning? Remember, it is always best to involve potential allies in the early stages of planning in order to offer them full participation in the work and create truly collective action.

5. *Select a strategy.*

Who does what when? Develop alternative plans so there are options. In this step the group has to figure out all the details, from what type of sandwiches to make to how to get to the park. Are there any local government restrictions? Is there a safety issue that needs to be taken into consideration? Whose kitchen can be used for making the sandwiches? Who will go to the store? Where will the money come from to buy the food? Try to cover all the steps in your planning.

6. *Develop and implement tactics.*

Tactics are the specific steps that make up the strategy. They include assigning actions to particular people, creating a time line, and scheduling future meetings for evaluating the progress of the plan. Be sure to include an end date for the project.

At this stage, the tasks generated in step five are assigned to the members of the group. An example of a schedule for a Saturday project might look something like this: the people who agreed to buy the food go to the store on Friday; everyone meets at the church Saturday morning at 9:00 A.M. to make the sandwiches; parents help drive the youth and the food to the park by 11:30 A.M.

7. *Evaluate the Project.*

Be sure to evaluate how things are going at every step. In evaluating the project, consider the following: How is the group functioning in terms of morale, efficiency, and the meaning of the task? What has been learned about social change and the personal growth that social responsibility brings? Has the project helped solve the problem? This is really more of an ongoing process than the other steps, but be sure to do it at the end of the project as well.

What relationships have formed that will continue to challenge injustice beyond the act of service itself? Focus on and acknowledge the hard work and effort that the youth have contributed, even if everything didn't go exactly as planned. Maybe the lemonade got spilled in the parking lot; maybe half the sandwiches had peanut butter without any jelly. The important thing is that the group made a difference in the lives of some homeless people. They learned more about people and circumstances outside of their normal understanding, and they worked together as a team to create that difference. Youth need to feel good about the work they do, even if it isn't perfect, or they will be less likely to try again.

Social action projects work best for youth groups if they are concrete, hands-on experiences with distinct beginnings and ends. Youth are motivated when they see the results of their work and feel that they have made a difference. It is hard to keep up enthusiasm for intangible, never-ending projects such as letter-writing campaigns. Projects that have been successful with youth groups include participating in a protest or rally, cleaning up the environment, collecting and delivering gifts for children in shelters, providing services for people with AIDS, and helping to build a new inner-city playground. The following resources can be very helpful when you are looking for social action projects for your group. A more thorough listing is available on the Council on International Education Exchange website, www.ciee.org. You can contact them at 7 Custom House Street, 3rd Floor, Portland, ME 04101, Tel.: (207) 553-7600.

UUA's Advocacy and Witness Staff Group
25 Beacon Street
Boston, MA 02108
Tel.: (202) 296-4672, ext. 10
Fax: (202) 296-4673
Email: A_W@uua.org
The primary responsibility of this staff group is to take Unitarian Universalist values out into the wider world and bring Unitarian Universalist per-

spectives to public debates on the issues of the day through media advocacy, partnerships with other religious and secular organizations, and empowerment of congregations. Within this staff group you will find the Office of Congregational Advocacy and Witness, the Holdeen India Program, the Office of Information and Public Witness, the Office of Interfaith Partnerships, the Office of International Relations, the Social Justice Internship Program, and the Washington Office for Advocacy.

UUA's Identity-Based Ministries Staff Group
25 Beacon Street
Boston, MA 02108
Tel: (617) 948-6475
This office is designed to provide programs and services to underserved people within our movement who are marginalized by disability, economic status, gender, race, or sexual orientation.

Just Works Program
Unitarian Universalist Service Committee
130 Prospect Street
Cambridge, MA 02139-1845
Tel: (617) 868-6600
This program offers summer work camps with hands-on projects to put faith into action. Provides service opportunities around the United States.

Unitarian Service Committee of Canada (USC)
56 Sparks Street
Ottawa, Canada K1P5B1
Tel.: (613) 234-6827
Volunteers can get involved in a variety of ways—by organizing public displays, contributing fundraising ideas and projects, coordinating special events in local communities, arranging presentations to schools and other community groups, or by working at the national office or one of the provincial offices.

American Friends Service Committee
1501 Cherry Street
Philadelphia, PA 19102
(215) 241-7275
This Quaker organization includes people of various faiths who are committed to social justice, peace, and humanitarian service. Its work is based on the Religious Society of Friends' (Quaker) belief in the worth of every person and faith in the power of love to overcome violence and injustice. Programs focus on economic justice, peacebuilding and demilitarization, social justice, and youth, in the United States, Africa, Asia, Europe, Latin America, and the Middle East, and at the United Nations (Geneva and New York).

Habitat for Humanity International
121 Habitat Street
Americus, GA 31709
Tel.: (229) 924-6935, ext. 2551 or 2552
Email: publicinfo@hfhi.org
This is the main headquarters, but Habitat for Humanity has many local groups. Youth work on a variety of projects geared toward providing decent housing for people. This organization has a strong ecumenical Christian base.

Volunteers for Peace
1034 Tiffany Road
Belmont, VT 05730
Tel.: (802) 259-2759
Email: vfp@vfp.org
This group serves to match Americans and Canadians with work camps abroad (especially in Europe) and matches overseas volunteers with work camps in the United States.

Youth Services Opportunities Project
15 Rutherford Place
New York, NY 10003
Tel.: (212) 598-0973
This Quaker-affiliated group offers weekend opportunities for service in New York City and its environs. Weekend projects are designed for high school and college-aged groups. Projects typically center on feeding the hungry and working with the homeless. The program also provides "alternative low-cost outings to New York" with low-cost accommodations.

Pike's Peak Justice and Peace Commission
29 South Institute Street
Colorado Springs, CO 80903
Tel.: (719) 632-6189
Email: staff@pikespeakjusticeandpeace.org

This educational nonprofit organization works on nonviolence training and philosophy and provides formative experience on social justice issues. Volunteers provide administrative and program support.

Worship

Don't be afraid to include worship in your youth group. Given the opportunity, youth will find their own ways of expressing their spirituality. Create rituals to help build and solidify your group. Establish a coming-of-age service. Develop a ritual for youth graduating from high school. Welcome new youth with a ritual when they are ready to officially join the group.

Rituals for lesser occasions are equally important. Opening and closing rituals help youth to define their time together as special and separate from the rest of their lives. Openings can be as simple as lighting a chalice and requesting silence. You could add a reading, which you choose at first; later you can encourage youth to select their own readings. Many groups follow the opening with a check-in, where people speak briefly about what is going on in their lives. Because people have few times in their lives when they can speak without interruption, the opportunity to just say how they are can be a meaningful and spiritual event for all. Closings can be as simple as a group hug, a song, or passing a squeeze. This sense of closure is important to participants and can be a helpful life practice. By establishing ways to create endings you can help youth understand the importance of closure.

A more traditional expression of spirituality can take the form of a worship service. Youth worship usually does not look like adult worship. There is seldom a sermon, the youth usually sit in a circle, and they often incorporate chants, movement, and sharing into the service. One of the most enjoyable types of worship is the "My Favorite Worship" service. Ask your group to brainstorm the elements of worship that they like most. Each youth will be responsible for one of those elements. Allow a break for people to put these elements together and then bring the group back together for a worship service composed of things everyone likes best. Unfortunately, YRUU worship and Unitarian Universalist services are sometimes vulnerable to a tradition of cultural misappropriation. Try to encourage youth to give voice to the context and background of practices used in worship from different cultures.

Rev. Jaco ten Hove offers the following list of "Elements to Help Make Your Worship Complete," with the foundational elements forming the base of the pyramid:

music
silence
sharing
emotion
movement
imagination
a distinct mood
an appeal to the senses
peaceful centeredness
grounding in the earth
a sense of the individual in the community

Youth can use these worship skills to lead services in your congregation. Worship is a good place for youth to share with the larger community the means of expression and caring that they have enjoyed in their youth group. Having a youth-led service is good for building the youths' self-esteem and for making the congregation aware of the youths' spirituality. Youth often bring a refreshing and deeply spiritual touch to worship. Worship can also be a great community-building mechanism at conferences.

If your youth group isn't used to worship and/or is really turned off by the idea, then take them to a conference. Worship is an important element of district conferences, and your youth group will see an excellent example of youth-led worship there. Many youth groups come back from conferences inspired to make worship a regular experience in their own group.

To help your youth group get started, consider using the following ideas for worship: addictions, balance, belonging, circles, cooperation, death and life, Dr. Seuss, earth, family issues, freedom, friendship, gender, healing, intergenerational sharing, moon phases, music, nature, non-violence, peace and war, percussion, self- confidence, self-respect, sensations, sexuality, silence, stereotypes, stewardship, home, Taoism, transitions, the universe, water.

Learning

There probably isn't a youth group meeting in which someone doesn't learn something. Social action, leadership, worship—and even the most social of youth group gatherings—provide learning opportunities. Curricula are great resources for your youth group. (See page 59 in this handbook for curricula that have been used successfully with youth groups.) But using a curriculum does not create a balanced youth program. Make sure, if you are using one, that you have other types of programming as well.

YRUU is a great place for discussion. You can bring in speakers to discuss issues youth are particularly interested in. Ask a parishioner with a special skill or hobby to come and share it with the group. Youth groups have done everything from learning to sail, to studying the history of Unitarian Universalism in Transylvania, to developing their own photo exhibit. Find out what your group is interested in and what your congregation has to offer.

The UUA has a long history of valuing a young person's right to comprehensive sexuality education. Some may question whether sexuality is an appropriate topic for church, but sexuality is a spiritual issue. If we do not provide our youth with knowledge about their bodies, pride in who they are, respect for others, and skills to live out their values in loving and healthy relationships, we are not raising our youth to be healthy, responsible, spiritually whole human beings. Youth are seldom given the opportunity to talk about sex in an honest, respectful manner with their peers; to ask the questions they are curious about and receive truthful answers; or to express their feelings, hopes, and fears in a supportive environment.

Because many of the sexuality education programs in schools today—when they are offered—are incomplete or have been developed by the Religious Right, it is even more important that we provide this opportunity in our churches. Contact the UUA Bookstore for the most current sexuality education program, and the Youth Office for information about training leaders for the program.

Congregational Involvement

The final aspect of a balanced program is creating opportunities for the youth to interact with the larger congregation. A good youth program will be a catalyst for creating an intergenerational community in our congregations. Youth will thrive in their leadership development if they feel that they are empowered by the whole congregation, not just the youth advisor. Youth have talents, perspectives, and leadership skills that can be valuable in every aspect of congregational life. Advisors can help make this happen in two ways. The first is to encourage youth to take part in the activities of the larger church. Many youth may not realize that they have something to offer the worship committee, but with your encouragement they might help transform the way your congregation worships. You might encourage youth with musical talent to join the choir or the music ministry team. You can also can advocate for youth with church leaders. As an adult, you can help open doors for youth participation and leadership by introducing youth to committee chairs, by encouraging committees to invite youth into their membership, and by asking adult leaders to include youth in planning programs and events for the church community. If you would like more suggestions about how to get youth involved with the larger congregation, feel free to contact the Youth Office.

Leadership

One of YRUU's most valuable gifts is the leadership opportunities it provides to young people. There are few organizations in our society that encourage teenagers to take responsibility for their own programs, and fewer still in which young people can gain the skills they need to succeed. Youth groups empower youth to express what they think and feel, to learn to work together, and to live out their values in the world.

Leadership in YRUU may not look exactly like the models of leadership you are used to working with in other parts of your life. Youth groups and YRUU governing bodies tend to rely more on consensus than on voting, and more on collaboration than on hierarchy. It can be a challenge for an advisor to adjust to this different style of leadership.

Leadership Styles

In our culture, the most common leadership model is a hierarchy, also known as *directive leadership*. If a youth group uses this model, the adult advisor plans and directs all the activities for the group. The benefits of this style are that things will run "smoothly" and young people will learn the "right" way to do things. But there are also some real drawbacks.

In a directive leadership, you will be exhausted because you are doing all the work, and youth will become less motivated and enthusiastic about programs they don't help create and lead. Sharing the responsibility is more likely to lead to an equal amount of work for everyone and a shared investment in the project. Although you may think you know the "best" way to accomplish something based on your past experience, programs can surprise you when they benefit from a youth's fresh eye and energy.

In *nondirective leadership*, the advisor allows group members to explore and find their own solutions. Youth are encouraged to take ownership of and responsibility for their own programming. The role of the nondirective advisor is to offer support and to advise the youth when appropriate. But the most important value of nondirective leadership is that the youth learn a great deal more by experiencing things themselves.

Think about how you learned to ride a bicycle. When you watched an older person ride a bicycle you saw how it was done, but you really learned to ride a bicycle when you got on and did it yourself. As an advisor, you may want to coach youth about how to improve their bike-riding skills. Or you may want to stand by until they have fallen a few times and wait for them to ask you for some tips. Either way, they will learn more if you don't do their riding for them.

Youth group projects offer youth the opportunity to fail without disastrous consequences. Solving small problems when things don't go as planned helps them develop techniques for handling larger ones later on. This is wonderful training in the leadership skills that youth will need throughout their lives.

As an advisor, one of the best things you can do is to hold your tongue and count to ten. Then count to ten again. This can be very difficult: There is nothing harder than listening to a group try to solve a problem you have solved successfully yourself. Sometimes it may feel as if you are going to bite right through your tongue.

Yet, given time and patience, the group may well arrive at the very solution you were going to suggest. And they will feel much better about the solution if they have been allowed to come up with it themselves. If you practice this technique, you give the youth the opportunity to lead themselves. You boost their self-esteem and help them learn that they are competent individuals.

Facilitating

If you are an advisor to a group that hasn't yet developed skills for reaching their goals, you may have to show the group how it can be done. Let's say your group has had no experience in planning and running an overnight event. Instead of planning, organizing, and "doing" the event yourself, see if you can model inclusiveness as you coach and guide the group. In other words, try to be a *facilitator* for the group, rather than the leader.

Know Your Role

Remember that a facilitator is neither a spectator nor a direct participant; nor is she or he a dictator. A good facilitator is like a midwife, guiding the group with a minimum amount of pain. A good facilitator also manages stress well. Some conflict is inevitable, but a facilitator can make use of the energy it generates to bring the group to creative, satisfying solutions.

Be Aware of the Group

As a facilitator, you must consider yourself responsible for the group members' feelings and the outcome of the meeting. Be aware of the needs of the group. If people are tired or stressed out, encourage a short break or an energizing activity. If people are hyperactive and rowdy, don't be afraid to assert yourself and take a little more control than usual (but do try to focus all that energy on resolving the issue).

Be Attentive to Power Relationships

The most successful facilitation styles match the expectations of the group. If the group expects or needs a great deal of guidance but receives only a little, the group will flounder. But if the group needs more independence than the leader is allowing, there will be a "turf fight" for more power. Remember, it is not your job to solve the group's problems. Your job is to create the environment in which your group can effectively solve problems on its own.

The following pointers can help you facilitate the meeting successfully:

- Watch how people arrange themselves.
- Make sure that they can see each other.
- Watch the energy level of the group.
- Have quick re-energizing games to play.
- Share responsibilities.
- Include those who are left out.
- Be aware of and try to address power dynamics due to gender and race.
- Don't use your position to push your own views.

Consensus

Consensus is a decision-making process that encourages inclusiveness, discourages divisiveness, and gives each member of the group ownership of the outcome. When working to achieve consensus:

- Make sure each member of the group understands the issue at hand. Encourage questions for clarification.
- Encourage those with pertinent background information to share it.
- Stay focused on the issue during discussion.
- Listen to others' points of view and define your own.
- Evaluate previous actions, methods, or decisions that relate to the current issue.
- Avoid putting other people down or negating others' ideas in order to get your own across.
- Encourage individuals to argue for what they believe in. Make sure that you are listening to others and treating their ideas, even those you don't support, with respect and consideration.

When the issues have been discussed as much as possible, the group may find itself in one of the following three situations:

- *The group is ready for resolution.*
  The facilitator can state what she or he believes is the consensus of the group, then ask for questions and discussion. "It seems to me we have a consensus. Is that the case?" Remember that silence does not always mean yes.
- *The group has reached a crucial question.*
  If the group has reached an impasse because a crucial question that needs to be examined, take the time to examine it. Brainstorming and/or discussion can be useful tools here for finding answers and solutions. No matter what kind of ideas you want to generate as a group, brainstorming is a great technique. Markers and newsprint are some of the few required tools of the advisor trade. Have one person facilitate by writing all ideas on paper. The only rules for brainstorming are not to limit the answers and not to comment on others' suggestions. Look at all possibilities. Suppose you are talking about possible events for your group. A trip to Disneyland is probably impractical, a trip to the moon impossible. But don't limit your brainstorming! You can edit

later—don't let anyone block the creativity of the group by saying, "We can't go to the moon!" Brainstorming may help you find new solutions to old problems. Brainstorming the steps to planning an overnight event may seem obvious to you, but remember that this is new for your group. Be open to the possibility that they have thought of a step you haven't considered. Once the list has been generated, then you can go back and evaluate. The group can then be more critical, eliminating ideas that obviously won't work and reaching consensus on the ideas that remain.

- *The group is stuck.*
  When the issue has been discussed and the group is polarized, exhausted, frustrated, out of time, or any combination of the above, something must be done. The skills and creativity of the facilitator come into play. Take charge, but leave the power with the group. Ask critical questions. Help the group redirect any energy being spent in frustration with individuals toward solving the problem. Be open to process suggestions from the group. Brainstorm, assign the problem to a subcommittee for further examination, ask each person to share her or his feelings on the issue, and/or take a break (however brief). Sometimes people who are blocking consensus will concede, provided that their concerns are noted in writing with the text of the resolution. Watch carefully for the buds of consensus. Finally, beware of falling into the trap of heatedly discussing a meaningless point for hours. Be prepared to ask the group, "Do we really need to be talking about this right now?" If you have tried your best to achieve consensus but haven't found it, don't be afraid to take a break and go on to the next agenda item. Just agree on a time to return to the difficult issues.

Once you have established a working model of facilitation with your group, encourage the youth to take turns being facilitators. When youth are empowered, they blossom and grow. Shy, introverted people become leaders. They gain new skills for working with others as they learn about facilitation, group dynamics, and leadership, and as their self-confidence grows. They learn how to work with adults and other people in authority and how to work for issues that are important to them. They develop an identity as a Unitarian Universalist young adult. When you promote youth leadership, you are providing youth with gifts for a lifetime.

Creating a Safe Group

While providing youth with the opportunity to grow, develop, and express their Unitarian Universalist values, you need to ensure that you, the youth, and the congregation are as safe as possible. No environment will be 100 percent safe, but there are certain measures that every youth group should take. Make use of the many resources you have available when questions come up—or better yet, before they come up. Talk to your religious educator, minister, other advisors, and/or the UUA Youth Office whenever you need support. Use appropriate written applications, screening procedures, and personal reference checks for all youth advisors and leaders. Check out the UUA web resources. Don't try to do it all alone! That's how advisors get themselves in trouble.

It's a good idea to keep a notebook in the church office or in your YRUU meeting place listing the youth in the group. Include information such as name, address, phone number, parent or guardian, parents' phone numbers, other emergency contacts, and any allergy and health considerations you should be aware of. We hope you will never experience a medical emergency during a meeting, but it's a good idea to have information available just in case.

If you go on any type of field trip or off-site event, be sure to obtain a signed parental permission slip for each youth who participates. This should include a medical release. If you don't have such a signed form, your congregation may be held liable for any accidents or injuries. A sample form is included in the Resources section of this handbook, but each congregation should develop one that meets its particular needs. Congregations should also have their lawyers check parental permission slips for relevance to state/province and local laws.

Make sure your congregation has developed a travel policy before taking the youth group on any outings. In many states, the church can be held liable for traffic accidents if the church was "providing transportation" to and from events. This generally includes car pools if they were organized through the youth group. In creating a policy, you should consider the following issues:

- Does the church have a copy of each driver's license and insurance card?
- Is it okay with parents if youth ride in cars driven by other youth?
- Do you have a policy requiring drivers to follow all traffic regulations, use seat belts, obey speed limits, etc.?
- Do you forbid smoking in vehicles with youth?
- Do you have a minimum sleep requirement for drivers returning from overnight events?

Document any incidents or reports of injuries or accidents and keep them on file. Use a standardized form and make sure incidents are reported to the religious educator and/or minister of your congregation.

Another transportation issue has to do with getting people home after meetings. Advisors should not be responsible either for taking youth home or waiting for parents to pick them up. If the meeting ends at 9:00 P.M. on Sunday night, it's unreasonable for you to still be there at 10:30 P.M. waiting for parents to pick youth up. Try to make your expectations clear in your advisor contract.

Preventing Abuse

Child abuse is defined as an act committed by a person in a position of trust—adult, older youth, teacher, leader—that harms or threatens to harm a young person's well-being or physical or mental health. The scope of the problem of child abuse is a challenge to all of us in religious communities. In 1996, Child Protective Service agencies determined that almost one million children were victims of substantiated or indicated child abuse or neglect. One in four girls and one in six boys will be sexually abused before they turn sixteen according to 1990 Federal Bureau of Investigation statistics. Of these victims, the vast majority—75 to 95 percent—know their abusers. Offenders are from all socioeconomic levels, ethnic groups, and educational backgrounds.

Ask your religious educator to provide training for youth staff and volunteers in basic first aid, child abuse prevention and reporting, universal precautions (handling bodily fluids and dealing with infectious diseases), and fire safety. Determine the process to be followed if there is an incident, disclosure, or accusation of abuse or neglect. Know your state or province laws on reporting abuse or neglect.

Power Dynamics

With your role as a youth group advisor comes a certain amount of power. Although you may find that power confusing or even unwelcome, it is unavoidable. You will have power by virtue of being older and because you have more experience, knowledge, and financial resources than the youth in your group. Power is not easily defined or recognized, let alone embraced. It can be viewed in three ways: power over, power with, and power within. "Power over" is often abusive, as when a teacher gets sexually involved with a student, when a boss uses his/her authority to silence employees, or when a spouse or parent physically or emotionally abuses a partner or child.

However, "power over" can also be used appropriately—as, for example, when a mother pulls her child out of the path of an oncoming car. Young people have experienced "power over" in their relationships with their parents, teachers, and other adults and authority figures. This has been an important part of their learning and development, teaching them about who they are and how they are expected to act.

But for youth to grow into responsible adults, they need to start making decisions on their own. As an advisor, you do not need to perpetuate the experience of "power over" that they have with other adults. Work with them instead in a "power with" model, in which we recognize youths' internal power or "power within." This "power within" is the inherent worth and dignity that every individual possesses, which is expressed through their own ideas, opinions, feelings, and decision-making.

But be aware and understand that power-vulnerability ratios are relative and contextual. A person has power and is vulnerable *in relation* to another person in a given context. An adult male heterosexual European-American youth advisor has many sources of power in relation to a female lesbian Latina youth. It's important to understand the power dynamics inherent in your youth advisor roles and relationships.

To work in a model of "power with" is to encourage youth leadership and consensual decision making. The "power with" model honors youths' voices. It helps them explore the ramifications of their behavior so that they learn to make good choices. It does not tell them what to do or when to do it but honors their choices even if we feel they might not be the best ones available.

This doesn't mean that an advisor should never step in to use his/her "power over" to influence the youth. Like the parent of the child who runs into the road, you should step in anytime you feel the youth are in imminent danger and use "power over" to ensure their safety. For example, if during a worship service the chalice accidentally set the curtains on fire, you would immediately grab the fire extinguisher and put it out. You would not wait for a youth to explore their options, collectively try to recall where the fire extinguisher is kept, read the instructions on how to use it, and then put out the fire. Once the danger has passed, you can turn the event into a "power with" situation. The youth could brainstorm ways to ensure this never happens again and decide how to make amends to the congregation and replace the curtains.

As the advisor, you are accountable for assessing the appropriate or inappropriate use of your power. Your age, experience, and the position the congregation has bestowed on you mean that you will always have more power than the youth. What you do with that power is your choice and responsibility.

Setting Personal Boundaries

Adults working with children and youth in the context of our Unitarian Universalist faith have a crucial and privileged role, one which may carry with it a great deal of power and influence. Whether acting as youth advisor, chaperone, childcare worker, teacher, minister, registrant at an adult/youth conference, or in any other role, the adult has a special opportunity to interact with our young people in ways that are affirming and inspiring to the young people and to the adult. Adults can be mentors to, role models for, and trusted friends of children and youth. They can be teachers, counselors, and ministers. Helping our children grow up to be caring and responsible adults can be a meaningful and joyful experience for the adult and of lifetime benefit to the young person.

While it is important that adults be capable of maintaining meaningful friendships with the young people they work with, adults must exercise good judgment and mature wisdom in using their influence with children and youth and refrain at all times from using young people to fulfill their own needs. Young people are in a vulnerable position when dealing with adults and may find it difficult to speak out when adults behave inappropriately.

In recruiting adult leaders, we need to look for adults with a special dedication to work with our young people in ways that affirm the UUA Principles. Good communication skills, self-awareness, understanding of others, sensitivity, problem-solving and decision-making skills, and a positive attitude are all important attributes. Additionally, we should seek persons who have a social network outside of their religious education responsibility in which to meet their own needs for friendship, affirmation, and self-esteem, and who are willing and able to seek assistance from colleagues and religious professionals when they become aware of a situation requiring expert help or intervention. It is ultimately the responsibility of the entire church or conference community, not just those in leadership positions, to create and maintain a climate that supports the growth and welfare of children and youth.

In January 1986, the UUA Board of Trustees appointed a committee to develop a code of ethics for persons working with children and youth. All advisors are required to read, sign, and abide by the following Code of Ethics. If your congregation hasn't asked you to do so, you should start the precedent yourself.

> Adults and youth who are in leadership roles are in a position of stewardship and play a key role in fostering spiritual development of both individuals and the community. It is, therefore, especially important that those in leadership positions be well qualified to provide the special nurture, care, and support that will enable youth to develop a positive sense of self and a spirit of independence and

responsibility. The relationship between young people and their leaders must be one of mutual respect, if the positive potential is to be realized.

There are no more important areas of growth than those of self-worth and the development of a healthy identity as a sexual being. Leaders play a key role in assisting youth in these areas of growth. Wisdom dictates that all those involved suffer damaging effects when leaders become sexually involved with young persons in their care; therefore, leaders will refrain from engaging in sexual, seductive, or erotic behavior with youth in the community. Neither shall they sexually harass or engage in behavior with youth which constitutes verbal, emotional, or physical abuse. Leaders shall be informed of this Code of Ethics and agree to it before assuming their role. In cases of violation of the Code, appropriate action will be taken.

Any form of sexual relationship between an advisor and a youth is inappropriate. This includes intimate physical contact, as well as verbal or emotional sexualization, such as flirting and sexual harassment. Youth are sensitive to the demands and innuendos of adults. Because they have rarely in their lives been given permission to say no to an adult, it's hard for them to do so. It's your job to put the needs and care of the youth first. If you hug someone and he or she feels uncomfortable or awkward, you have gone too far. Even if it's just an innocent hug, it doesn't matter: if the youth feels it's too much, it is.

As an advisor, you need to make sure that your emotional needs are met outside of the group. You must not expect the youth to fill voids in your life or help you through personal emotional struggles. We all derive benefits from working with youth; and for many of us, the work brings up some of our personal issues. This is normal. What you do with these feelings is of primary concern: Your personal issues should not become the group's issues.

Use your own network of friends, other advisors, the religious educator, and/or minister for support.

It may also sometimes be difficult to stay in your "adult" role as advisor. The youth in your group are looking for a friend and advisor, but they want you to be an adult one. If you think becoming an advisor is a chance to relive your youth, think again. This doesn't mean that you can't play games or participate with your group. It does mean that you should keep a certain distance or boundary between you and the youth. They will not be comfortable with you at the same level of intimacy that they share with each other.

Additionally, if youth make demands or requests that are inappropriate, or are too physically affectionate with you, it is up to you to set the boundaries. Be assertive. Ask questions; name the problem; state the consequences. Your assertiveness, using honest and direct language and making your voice and body language congruent, will enhance effective communication. Youth may be testing their own boundaries, but it is up to you to establish the limits.

One fairly safe method is to return demonstrations of affection only in kind. Don't hug until you are hugged, and then only at the level you received the hug. You may be the first adult to touch this youth outside of her or his family. There may be all sorts of other factors going on beneath the surface that you are not aware of. Respect everyone's boundaries and give people adequate space to respond as they need to.

This is an extremely important issue. Not only can you make things uncomfortable for the youth, but the situation can become awkward for you. While it is nearly impossible for youth to tell you if they are uncomfortable with your behavior, it is almost as hard for them to tell another adult about you. Once the issue has come up, it is difficult to hear and hard to resolve. Remind youth of their sexual rights and responsibilities (see *Our Whole Lives: Sexuality Education for Grades 7–9* and *Our Whole Lives: Sexuality Education for Grades 10–12*), and remember your own ethical rights and responsibilities.

Walk Your Talk

We all remember the old adage, "Do as I say, not as I do." It didn't work on us when we were young, and it doesn't work today. Whatever rules or behavior guidelines your youth group has set apply to you as well as the youth at all meetings and events. If the group decides on segregated sleeping at an overnight, you abide by that rule even if you are attending with your spouse or partner. If there is no smoking, you don't smoke. Legally you can smoke or drink or do as you please, but doing so breaks the trust and spirit of community you are trying so hard to create. You will not come across as a good role model. Try to set the same standards for everyone, including yourself.

Advisors are granted the opportunity to develop a unique relationship with youth. You are in relationship with them because you want to be, not because of kinship or profession. It is important for you to remember that as an advisor you are not their parent or their teacher, you are an advisor. You are not a baby-sitter or the congregation's police officer. Your role is not to be an authority figure. You are an adult friend who offers help, support, and guidance when needed.

Communication

Confidentiality is important for creating an environment of trust and support in a youth group. This doesn't mean that you never tell the religious educator or parents what the youth group is doing. You and the youth group are, after all, a part of the congregation. What you don't talk about are the personal events and feelings that individuals share with the group. It's fine to say that the group went on a picnic. It's not okay to tell people that Rob, Kimbrin, and Sarah got into an argument at the picnic about who had the most difficult parents.

As an advisor, you should set up regular meetings with your religious educator and/or minister. They should be kept aware of what is happening in the youth group so they can better support you and the group's programs. Youth ministry is a team effort and no one should try to do it all alone.

While you don't want to share with the parents the specifics of what is said in the youth group, it is also important to keep them aware of what is happening. They are invested in strong youth programming or they would never have brought their children to be involved in the congregation. They can be among your best sources of support.

Send a letter to all the parents at the start of each semester and let them know what the youth group has planned for the coming weeks. If you need assistance in any areas, include a form at the bottom of your flyer asking for help. If you need drivers to an event, snacks brought for a meeting, or cookies baked for a fundraiser, find out what parents can provide. And it's important to build good relationships with all the parents. You don't want to be left doing everything yourself.

Reporting Abuse

The issue of confidentiality can become a crisis for you as well as the youth when you believe or know that a youth is being abused. Learn the definitions of abuse (physical abuse, sexual abuse, emotional abuse, and neglect) and harassment. Be familiar with possible indicators of abuse—behavioral clues and other warning signs—and what various levels of disclosure look and sound like. It's important for you to be able to describe acquaintance rape and sexual exploitation and to articulate respectful behaviors and "do-no-harm" ethics.

Every congregation should develop a procedure for reporting abuse and should train all church volunteers in these procedures. A congregation's professional religious educator is a "mandated reporter," required by law to report instances of suspected abuse. It is important for you to know and follow the reporting procedures in your congregation and at any host community/site you visit with your group. For more information on developing such a procedure, please refer to *Reducing the Risk of Child Sexual Abuse in Your Church* by Hammar, Klipowicz, and Cobble, published by Church Law and Tax Report in 1993. This book can be found in every UUA district office. Another valuable resource is *Creating Safe Congregations: Toward an Ethic of Right Relations,* edited by Patricia Hoertdoerfer and William Sinkford, published by the UUA in 1997 and available from the UUA Bookstore.

Although youth group advisors are seldom "mandated reporters," you nevertheless have a moral mandate to protect youth. If you know of a youth who is in physical or emotional danger, you need to respond in a way that is best for that youth. If you have an established procedure and know your reporting obligations, you can develop clear statements that don't engage in denial, minimization, or blame, and that honor your responsibilities and accountabilities.

Consult your congregation's attorney (and board president, minister, and religious educator), your district staff, and your insurance company when developing such procedures. Contact the UUA's Lifespan Faith Development staff group for a copy of the Safety/Abuse Clearinghouse Packet, the pamphlet *Honoring the Children: What We Can Do to Prevent Child Abuse,* and information on the curricula *Our Whole Lives: Sexuality Education for Grades 7–9* and *Our Whole Lives: Sexuality Education for Grades 10–12.*

Let your youth group know the types of things you won't keep confidential. When you develop your covenant as a group and the issue of confidentiality comes up, tell them, "If you tell me something that I feel indicates that you are in danger, I am going to have to tell someone else." That's part of your "do-no-harm" ethics. In addition, every time your group starts a discussion in which confidentiality is named as a rule, remind your group of what the limits are. Youth have a right to know what will happen if they reveal that they have been abused or are in danger of abuse.

If you do need to break a confidence that was shared in the group, then pull that youth aside and tell her or him, "I know that when you shared your information you asked that no one talk about your experience. But as your advisor I am concerned that you are in danger. I feel I need to tell Reverend Mays about your situation. Would you like to go with me to meet with her?" By informing the youth of your need to tell and inviting her or him to join you, you are not leaving the youth in a powerless position.

Your job as an advisor is not to be a therapist to your youth group. You are not there to fix their problems; you are there as a concerned friend. As such, be as honest and sincere as you can. Talk with your youth group about issues of abuse, rape, suicide, intimacy, and trust. Provide them with resources such as the phone numbers for hot lines and the names of youth agencies. Don't try to be more to the youth than you are able to be or than is appropriate.

How to Support Youth Advisors

If your religious educator or minister gave you this handbook, you might want to give it back so she or he can read this chapter. Make sure that whoever recruited you has not just sent you off to be with the youth with no support other than this handbook. Ministry with youth is a team effort. You should have the ongoing support of your religious educator, minister, youth/adult committee, religious education committee, parents, and board of trustees. They should all read this manual, or at least this chapter.

Often congregations are so relieved to find people willing to lead our youth groups that they forget the high-risk position we put our youth, advisors, and congregations in when we don't provide adequate screening, training, supervision, and safety policies. Taking a few extra steps in each of these areas will ensure that we provide the safest experience possible for our youth.

Creating an Advising Team

No advisor should be working alone with youth. Youth groups need a team of competent, committed adults if they are to have the leadership and continuity they need to flourish. If you have more than one adult working with the youth at all times, each advisor can have a week off now and then when they need a break. And if one adult has to stop advising, the whole program doesn't come to a halt. One advisor trying to do it all will rapidly lead to advisor burnout.

Having more than one advisor is also helpful for the youth. It is too much to ask the entire youth group to relate to just one adult. If you have a team, it is more likely that each youth will find at least one adult with whom she/he can make a special connection.

Adults frequently have concerns about youth that are based on previous experiences in their lives: I'll have to do everything . . . . My teenage years were hell . . . . I hate being parental . . . . Teenagers are loud and messy . . . . I won't be able to relate to them . . . .

Most of these concerns have little or nothing to do with YRUU youth groups. They are about our own sometimes painful adolescence, or they are based on vague generalizations of who teenagers are today. People make assumptions about youth because they don't know them as individuals. The more the adults in your congregation are exposed to youth, the easier it will be to break down this prejudice.

Adults can assist in advising in ways other than working with a weekly youth group. They can be advisors at conferences or for special field trips, and their time commitment can be as large or as limited as they like.

Great Ideas for Recruiting Youth Group Advisors

The process for recruiting advisors should involve input from the youth, the religious educator, the youth/adult committee if there is one, and the minister(s). Unfortunately, so few candidates usually respond that there is little opportunity to pick and choose. Here are some suggestions to help you get as many qualified applicants as possible:

- *Be specific about your expectations.*
  Prepare a job description so potential advisors know what they are committing to. They will be much more likely to agree if they know exactly what is expected of them and if the job isn't overwhelming.
- *Recruit more than one advisor.*
  Develop an advising team. People are more likely to agree if they know that all the work won't rest on their shoulders.
- *Extend a personal invitation.*
  Many people need to be asked, and they will appreciate your confidence in their ability. Others may not even be aware that an opportunity to advise the youth group exists, unless you tell them about it.
- *Put an ad in the church newsletter.*
  Advertising may bring qualified applicants out of the woodwork. It may also bring people you didn't want to know about. If you do recruit this way, make sure that you implement a detailed screening process to weed out candidates inappropriate for working with youth.
- *Arrange a testimonial.*
  Have current advisors, youth, former advisors, etc., "testify" from the pulpit about their positive experiences.
- *Take a survey.*
  Ask adults in the congregation what they would like to contribute to youth programs. Pass out a checklist with everything from baking cookies for a fundraiser, to attending a conference, to serving as a youth advisor. You probably will get many offers of help with the smaller jobs, but you also may find a couple of good candidates for youth group advisors.

- *Get more adults involved in smaller projects.*
  Help adults get their feet wet without making a long-term commitment. Once they get to know the youth, become interested in their lives, and feel less intimidated by them, they may volunteer for the bigger jobs.
- *Recruit parents.*
  Even though having parents as advisors can present some problems, they are often the people most interested in good youth programming for your church. (See "YRUU and the Youth Advisor" for more information about parents as advisors.)
- *Pay your advisors.*
  Sometimes the extra income can make the difference in convincing someone to commit to being a youth advisor. This is especially true for graduate students or people who are supporting themselves with several part-time jobs. If you can't pay your advisors, make sure you at least have money budgeted so that their expenses for advising are reimbursed. It should not cost anyone anything to be an advisor!
- *Offer support.*
  Have a budget line item to provide advisors with resources such as this handbook, books on games, activities, leadership development, etc. Send them to trainings, retreats, and other events at the church's expense.

Choosing Youth Group Advisors

Before recruiting, make sure you are clear about the procedure you will use to select your youth group advisors. Who will choose them—the youth group, the youth/adult committee, the religious educator, the religious education committee, an ad hoc advisor search committee, or a combination of the above? What information will you solicit from each candidate? (See the sample Advisor Application on page 56 of this handbook.)

We recommend that you involve some youth in the selection process; we also advocate that the youth group have the final say. Once you've selected your advisors, establish a one- or two-month trial period, after which you can solicit feedback from the group and the advisors to see if the combination is working well.

When recruiting individuals, make sure they understand they are not guaranteed the position, but will need to go through the established application procedure. Even if you have only one or two applicants, don't automatically give them the position without going through the procedure. Check references, interview them, and make sure that they are a good fit for the youth group. If this procedure seems complicated for a position that is hard enough to fill as it is, remember that when congregations fill advisor positions out of desperation and don't take the time to follow a simple application procedure, they may end up recruiting inappropriate adults.

Ideally, each applicant should be interviewed by the youth/adult committee or an ad hoc committee of youth and adults established to select advisors. Even if you know the applicants well, check references to get someone else's point of view. Some congregations require that an individual attend the congregation for at least six months before applying for a youth advisor position. If your congregation or youth group is committed to anti-racism work, ask applicants about their experience with racial identity and anti-racism work and let them know that they will be expected to participate in anti-racism workshops.

Training

Youth advisors will benefit from a training session geared specifically to them. The UUA's Youth Office has youth advisor trainers in every district. Ideally, each district office will have a list of available advisor trainers as well as a *Youth Advisor Training Planning Guide.*

Once you have selected and trained your youth group advisors, don't leave them to flounder with no support. Establish regular meetings with the religious educator, youth/adult committee, and/or religious education committee. It is a good idea to meet occasionally with your religious education professional to discuss how the adult advisor is doing. Don't leave advisors to handle everything themselves. Provide supervision to make sure that everything is going smoothly and provide support and assistance when needed.

Contracts

A contract is a useful tool to help clarify what is expected of the advisor, even if you decide not to call it anything as formal as a contract. The document can spell out how many times the advisor will meet with the youth group each month, what expenses are reimbursable, how many weekend conferences or retreats the advisor is expected to attend each year, how often she/he will meet with the religious educator, when she/he is responsible for transportation, what training and support the congregation will provide, how long her or his term as advisor will be, and other important information.

Make sure your contract includes the Code of Ethics for Adults Working With Youth (see "Creating a Safe Group"). Discuss what this Code of Ethics means with each advisor before he/she signs the contract. For a sample contract, see the Resources section at the end of this handbook.

Advisors at Conferences

Every conference should have someone coordinating the adults. This person is responsible for making sure that they know which advisors are attending, all advisors have directions, and the advisors know what to do.

If you are sponsoring a conference, send all the new advisors a welcome letter or flyer describing their role and telling them what to expect at the conference. You can find useful information about conferences in the UUA Youth Office resource "How to Be a Con Artist," available online at www.uua.org/YRUU.

All advisors at every conference should sign the Code of Ethics (see "Creating a Safe Group"). Discuss this code at the start of the conference to make sure the adults understand and agree with it.

Hold an adult orientation the first night of the conference. Use this time to allow the adults to get acquainted, talk about their roles at the conference, and express their fears or concerns about being an advisor. Be sure to give the new advisor plenty of support. A first conference for an adult can be as scary as it would be for a new youth. However, adults are much less likely to admit it—especially to youth. Help other new advisors to understand their role, talk about their concerns, and have fun!

Be sure to send all advisors a thank-you note after the conference so they will feel appreciated.

The Gifts of YRUU

One of the best ways to explore the riches of strong youth programming is to look at what individuals have said about YRUU:

"YRUU has been a sanctuary full of surprises and growth. It has been a place where I could feel welcome and at home and, in turn, welcome others. The same acceptance, safety, and comfort were there whether I was at an intense conference with ninety other crazy UUs or with all eight members of my local youth group."

—Rachel Reed, age twenty

"YRUU is a spiritual source for me. Long talks in the middle of the night and the worship help me get centered on my own life. It has also given me everlasting memories and an everlasting spiritual search of my own."

—Alison Purcell, age eighteen

"As a junior high student and growing Unitarian, I became very confused about my identity. YRUU gave me the strength to be myself and the courage to be a leader.

Seven years later I can honestly say I would be a different person at a different place in my life if it weren't for this organization!"

—Vanessa Wilcox, age twenty

"YRUU has let me grow and has allowed me to develop my own beliefs. The members of YRUU have always accepted my opinions and feelings, even if they don't agree with them."

—Marki Sveen, age fourteen

"The reason YRUU inspired me to keep coming back again and again and again was worship. Nowhere else in my largely secular daily life did both large and small groups of people come together in overt spiritual union and exploration. This is what made YRUU ultimately so meaningful to me."

—Marc Lousteau, age eighteen

"Nothing in my life has affected me more than my experience in YRUU. It helped me be the person I really am."

—Rob Cavenaugh, age twenty

"Being an advisor for YRUU has expanded my mind, enhanced my vision, and blessed my spirit. I carry their images and voices in my heart."

—Edith Parker, age sixty

Youth Programs for Our Future and Our Present

We all know that the youth of today are the adults of tomorrow. Youth who have valuable youth group experiences and identify themselves as Unitarian Universalists throughout their teen years are more likely to stay in the movement. By contributing to YRUU, you contribute directly to the future of Unitarian Universalism.

There is a value to our future world in helping youth to be caring, concerned, and committed. What we strive for in our congregations and our lives is a future with peace, justice, human dignity, and genuine concern for others. These young people with whom you are choosing to spend your time will determine what the future looks like in your congregation, community, and world.

And our youth are not only our future: They have important insights and perspectives for our faith right now. As an advisor, you are in a unique position to help integrate UU youth into the life of our faith. The more deeply connected our youth are with our congregations, our districts, and our Association, the more likely they are to stay involved as adults.

Please remember that the suggestions in this manual on how to provide Unitarian Universalist youth with the best possible programming are only ideas and jumping-off points. You can and will do it differently. Every congregation, district, youth group, and individual youth has its own needs, and there is no one right way to be a youth group advisor.

Above all, advisors need to be themselves, to model for youth how you navigate the world, how you live out your Unitarian Universalist values, and how you seek your highest potential. If you set a good example, there is a good chance the youth will follow it. Be honest and genuine with the youth you advise and they will love and trust you. You may make some lifelong friends, too.

Resources

Glossary

Learn to speak the language. The following is a current list of jargon that is used by YRUU across the continent.

Adult coordinator: Typically the person—sometimes a youth, sometimes an adult—who recruits adults for a conference, facilitates orientation and/or daily meetings for adults at the conference, and acts as a resource for adults.

Anti-racism: Anti-racism workshops expand the traditional concept of racism as personal prejudice to include institutional and cultural racism. They often include information on racial-identity development, including internalization of superiority and inferiority, and provide caucuses so that white people and people of color may separately address their own internalization issues (see *caucus*). Anti-racism workshops also often include information on institutional organizing and transformation.

Caucus: Same-identity group used at conferences and anti-racism trainings to explore identities, both privileged and oppressed. For example, an anti-racism training may have caucuses for white youth and youth of color.

Chaplain: The youth or adult who acts as a minister or spiritual guide at a conference or on a retreat. At large gatherings, consider having a female chaplain, a male chaplain, a GBLT chaplain, and a chaplain of color.

Check-in: Process at the beginning of a meeting in which people say how they are doing or how their week has been, or share current concerns. Check-in sometimes includes an icebreaker, such as name the vegetable you think your personality is most like, what color underwear you are wearing, etc.

Closing: A ritual or method by which you create closure for an event, worship, or meeting.

Closing circle: A common closing ritual for YRUU events in which participants form a circle.

Coffee house: A talent show that includes telling jokes, reading poetry, performing skits, singing songs, etc.

Con: A conference. In some districts, also called a *mini-con* or *rally*.

Conference Affairs Committee: Although it goes by different names in different districts, this committee is charged with responding to any rule infractions, crises, or conflicts that arise during the course of a conference. Made up of a few elected youth and adults, it is convened only if the need arises.

Consensus: The decision-making process by which all parties agree on a solution or recommendation.

CU²C² (Council of Unitarian Universalist Camps and Conferences): Organization of Unitarian Universalist camp sites, conference centers, and regularly occurring conferences. Many have programs specifically designed for youth.

C*UUYAN (Continental UU Young Adult Network): Grassroots young adult organization for eighteen- to thirty-five-year-olds. Sponsors annual spiritual conference called Opus and business and leadership development conference called Concentric.

District staff: All districts have a district executive, either lay or ordained; many have a program consultant, who focuses on religious education and youth programming. The district executives and program consultants are jointly employed by the UUA and the district and are a great resource for help in developing youth programming.

Dean: The leader or leaders responsible for coordinating the staff of a conference. Some districts use youth and adult co-deans.

District office: Every UUA district has an office that provides services for congregations and district programming. This office is staffed with a district executive; some also have a program consultant, who may focus on religious education or youth programming. The office usually has a library with resources that can be helpful in developing youth programs.

DRE (director of religious education): Person in charge of religious education programs at your local congregation. The DRE's responsibilities may include religious education for all ages (lifespan) or only for children and youth.

DRUUMM (Diverse & Revolutionary Unitarian Universalist Multicultural Ministries): Created in 1998, DRUUMM is an affiliate organization of the UUA that supports and advocates for people of color. DRUUMM runs events for multiracial families; leadership development for people of color and local and district groups; and activities for people of color at General Assembly and other national conferences.

DYSC (district youth steering committee): Another name for a district youth/adult committee.

Energy monitor: Person who keeps tabs on the energy or emotional climate of a meeting or conference, presenting short games or songs to re-energize the group at low points. See *energy break*.

Energy break: A song, dance, ritual, or break to allow people to get rid of negative energy.

Facilitator: Person responsible for organizing and leading a meeting.

Fishbowl: An exercise in which people sit in two circles, one inside the other. The outside circle gives written questions to the members of the inside circle, who discuss the questions among themselves while the outside circle listens. Those in the outside circle do not speak. This is a great process for groups who need to increase their understanding of one another in a nonthreatening or noncompetitive manner. For example, youth and adults, gays and straights, etc.

Foof or Floof (also spelled PHUUF): Blowing on someone's belly. This practice has declined over the years as more people see it as an activity that forces the recipient into a situation he or she is not comfortable with.

GA (General Assembly): Annual business meeting of the UUA.

Journey Toward Wholeness: The UUA's anti-racism and diversity initiative, started by a 1996 General Assembly resolution titled "Toward an Anti-racist Unitarian Universalist Association."

Jubilee World: Anti-racism trainings offered by the UUA for congregations.

Junior advisor: A young adult, under the age of twenty-five, who serves as an advisor while being mentored or supervised by an adult advisor.

Leadership Development Conference: A conference where youth and adults learn how to become leaders in YRUU and how to support dynamic youth programming in their congregations and districts.

LRY (Liberal Religious Youth): Unitarian Universalist youth movement that was the predecessor to YRUU.

Mailbags: Small paper bags that conference attendees decorate and label with their names. They are hung on a wall at conferences or other events to receive notes and treasures from other conferees.

MRE (minister of religious education): Minister who is generally responsible for the religious education programs in a congregation.

Networker: Someone who helps pull others of like experience together. An advisor networker helps advisors connect and share ideas.

One shots: A one-time workshop at a conference, lasting for only one to three hours.

Opening: A ritual or event that establishes the beginning of a meeting, helping people to gather and focus. Often consists of a reading, song, or chalice lighting.

Orientation: Held the first night of a conference to announce rules, events, procedures, and other information about the conference.

Pop: What half the continent calls soft drinks.

Religious educator: The person in your congregation responsible for religious education programs. She/he could be a director of religious education, minister of religious education, or religious education coordinator, or hold any one of a number of other titles.

SA (social action): Events, programs, and issues involving political or moral positions of conscience.

SAC (social action contact): Person in charge of communicating and developing social action events on a district or local level.

Secret buddy: Sometimes called a *mystery friend.* This is someone at a conference who sends you notes and little presents, and whose identity is not revealed until the end of the conference.

Sensorium: A workshop designed to delight the senses. Includes soft music, food, massage, etc.

Soda: What the other half of the continent calls soft drinks.

Spirit circle: Morning gathering at a conference. Announcements, songs, and other important things happen during a spirit circle.

Tonic: What a few people in New England call soft drinks.

Touch group: A small group of six to ten participants at a conference, facilitated by a touch group leader. This smaller group allows more people to get to know one another on a more intimate basis. Touch groups don't necessarily "touch," but will play games or participate in other activities to help the group bond.

UUA (The Unitarian Universalist Association of Congregations): Provides resources and services for member congregations. Headquarters are in Boston.

UU UNO (Unitarian Universalist United Nations Office): Organization that represents Unitarian Universalists at the United Nations. This office and the UUA Youth Office plan an annual conference at the United Nations in New York for youth ages fifteen to seventeen.

UUYAN (Unitarian Universalist Young Adult Network): Name for many local and district organizations for Unitarian Universalists ages eighteen to thirty-five.

Vegan: A vegetarian who does not eat any animal products, including eggs, dairy products, or meat.

Warm fuzzies: Good feelings, often in the form of notes or sweet things left in your mailbag at a conference.

Week-long: A workshop that meets for about two hours every day during a week-long conference.

Workshop: A session on a topic. It can be anything from crafts to politics, serious to silly, energetic to lazy.

YAC (youth/adult committee): The committee in charge of youth programs within a district or church. A ratio of one adult to every three youth is recommended. Has other names such as *youth council, steering committee, youth board,* etc.

YACM (Young Adult and Campus Ministry), formerly YAMs (Young Adult Ministries): UUA office that assists in serving the needs of people ages eighteen to thirty-five.

YCR (youth council representative): District representative to the Youth Council, the governing body of YRUU.

Youth caucus: Youth participants at the General Assembly who gather each day to decide their position on the business before the Association.

Youth Council: The continental YRUU governing body.

Youth Office: UUA office dedicated to supporting YRUU. A great resource for questions, problems, concerns, advice, general information, and good thoughts.

YPD (youth programs director): The director of the UUA's Youth Office.

YPS (YRUU programs specialist): A young adult who does a year-long internship at the UUA Youth Office. A YPS must be between the ages of sixteen and twenty-two when the internship begins.

YRUU (Young Religious Unitarian Universalists): An organization that provides youth group and district services for youth ages fourteen to twenty.

YRUU Steering Committee: Elected by Youth Council, the Steering Committee is the executive body of YRUU.

Permission Slip for a Fantabulistic Outing

Name: _____

Phone #: _____

Address: _____

_____

_____

_____

Health Insurance (name & number):

_____

_____

_____

I, _____ (please print), am the parent or legal guardian of
_____, who will be going on a Fantabulistic Outing with the Townville
UU Church YRUU group on Saturday, May 1, 2003. I hereby give my consent and authority for
the advisors accompanying the youth group to take any reasonable action to help ensure the
safety, health, and welfare of my child. I also give my consent for any necessary medical treatment,
including emergency surgical care if it is needed. I further understand that my child will be required
to follow the enclosed rules. A breach of these rules may result in my child being sent home at
the parent's expense, and prohibited from participating in future Townville YRUU events.

I understand my son/daughter will be driven to and from the event by

_____

In case of emergency on the above date, contact me at:

_____

Signature of Parent or Guardian: _____

Date: _____

Advisor Application

Name: _____

Address: _____

_____

_____

_____

Age: _____

How long have you been involved with this congregation?

If you were involved in another congregation before attending here, where was it?

What is it that interests you about becoming a youth group advisor?

What special skills, training, and education would you bring to the position?

What, if any, has been your previous experience working with youth?

If you have previous experience, what do you like most about working with youth?

What do you see your greatest challenge in youth work to be?

How do you understand youth empowerment?

What is your experience with anti-racism and anti-oppression work?

Name and explain any prior criminal conviction.

Please list two references, names and phone numbers, of people who are familiar with your ability to work with youth. Please list one youth if possible.

Youth Advisor Contract

The advisors for Sixth UU Church of Townville will:

- Attend three of the four youth group meetings each month, making sure there are always at least two advisors at every meeting. (They will arrange their schedules among themselves.)

- Attend one weekend overnight with the Sixth UU Youth Group and one district conference each year.

- Attend one continuing education program each year at the expense of the congregation. This could be an advisor training, Leadership Development Conference, New Games training, first aid training, or the like. Training must be approved beforehand by the religious educator.

- Meet monthly with the religious educator for supervision and support, and be an *ex-officio* member of the Youth/Adult Committee.

- Be reimbursed for all expenses involved with advising such as photocopying, mailings, snacks, transportation, etc. Annual expenses should not exceed $_____, and any single expenses exceeding $_____ should be approved beforehand by the Youth/Adult Committee.

- Advisors are asked to commit to the youth group for at least two years, but it is understood if an advisor is unable to fulfill that term. No advisor who is no longer happy in the position should continue working with the youth group . Advisors wishing to remain for longer than two years should discuss it with the religious educator and re-apply to the Youth/Adult Committee.

For More Information

The Youth Office has a number of resources available to assist you in working with youth. Their availability and format are always evolving. For the most current information, go to: www.uua.org/YRUU/resources.html. You may also call the Youth Office Assistant at (617) 948-4355 for details on the status of any resource. Address all general correspondence to:

UUA Youth Office
25 Beacon Street
Boston, MA 02108
Youth Office Hotline: (617) 948-4350
Fax: (617) 367-4798
E-mail: yruu@uua.org

Synapse: A YRUU Magazine by Youth for Everyone Synapse is the twice-yearly publication of YRUU. It is currently available online, although we anticipate that hard copies will be available to congregations and district offices. You may subscribe to an email list which provides updates about *Synapse* at www.uua.org/mailman/listinfo/synapse-L.

UUA Bookstore Resources

Call the UUA Bookstore at (617) 948-6102 or toll-free at (800) 215-9076 for ordering information. Order online at www.uua.org/bookstore.

Beyond Pink and Blue: Exploring Our Stereotypes of Sexuality and Gender by Tracey Robinson-Harris and Ritch Savin-Williams: This twelve-session curriculum for ages twelve to fifteen explores gender roles and identities, gender stereotypes, BGLT prejudices, and related issues.

Neighboring Faiths: Exploring World Religions with Junior High Youth by Christine Reed and Patricia Hoertdoerfer: Participants learn about their own faith by exploring other religious communities. For ages twelve to fourteen and adaptable for senior high youth.

Religion in Life: Boys and *Religion in Life: Girls:* Curricula for earning the religious emblem award offered by the UUA for Boy Scouts and Girl Scouts. These are also often used as coming-of-age curricula for UU youth who are not in scouting.

Our Whole Lives (OWL): The UUA's comprehensive sexuality education curriculum includes programs for grades 7–9 and for grades 10–12.

Race to Justice by Robin Gray and José Ballester: Fifteen sessions help youth ages twelve to fifteen explore racial justice and diversity through role-playing, games, and photography.

Youth Office Resources in Transition

All resources listed below are currently out of print, but are available from the Youth Office (address above). Send a letter with a check for the specified amount, made out to the UUA; we will send you a photocopy of the resource until we have the regular publication back in stock.

Coming-of-Age Resource
While neither the UUA nor the Youth Office have a "standard" coming-of-age curriculum, the Youth Office has collected several successful programs from various congregations.

Creating Safe Congregations: Toward an Ethic of Right Relations
Addresses preventing, recognizing, and responding to interpersonal abuse in congregations and communities.

Deep Fun: A Compendium of YRUU Games
It's just what it sounds like: an exciting combination of new and old games, divided into sections based on the Five Steps of Building Community. Everything from the silly to the profound. Sure to yield something for any group on just about any occasion. Another great thing to have for your district. *Deep Fun* is also available online at www.uua.org/yruu/resources.html.

Blessings to All Beings: A Youth Spiritual Anthology
The *Youth Spiritual Anthology* is a resource for creating youth worship. It includes homilies, sermons, poems, and readings about and by youth. This can be valuable for planning youth-led Sunday services as well.

The YRUU Songbook
This compendium of songs popular among YRUUers remains a great resource book for YACs at conferences. A limited supply of the accompanying audio tape are still available for an additional $5.

From YACs to SACs: A Guide to District Youth Programming
The essential resource for developing and supporting district youth programs. It is an invaluable guide for anyone organizing UU youth/young adult activities on a district level. This resource is also available online at www.uua.org/yruu/resources.html.

The Local Youth Group Handbook
The Local Youth Group Handbook is a collage of youth group experiences and practical suggestions for local youth group leaders and members. *The Handbook* contains a multitude of programming ideas for YRUU groups of any size.

Online Resources

The resources in this section are all available at www.uua.org/yruu/resources.html. You can purchase a hard copy of these resources in a single packet. Call the Youth Office for details.

Connect UU: An Online Directory of UU Youth and Young Adults
This online version of the shared youth and young adult database is a great way to make sure the Youth Office has your most current information. Get the latest news about events in your district, groups you might be interested in joining, ways to subscribe to YRUU email lists, and links to sites of YRUU interest.

Anti-Racism Movie Guide
This resource is a collection of descriptions and questions relating to four movies (*Mi Familia, American History X, SLAM,* and *Smoke Signals*). This guide is a great way for groups to start dialogue about racism.

How to Be a Con Artist: Youth Conference Planning Handbook for Unitarian Universalists
An extensive book-length youth conference planning guide.

A Code of Ethics for Adults and Older Youth
A generic sample of a code of ethics for adults and older youth involved in YRUU programming. Agreements such as these are typically filled out for youth events.

The Con-Etiquette Compromise: Creating Smoking Policies
This resource was designed to help YRUU groups create comprehensive smoking policies. There is no

policy regarding smoking at the continental level. It is up to each district to create a policy that is fair and equitable to both smokers and non-smokers.

Creating Rules in a Unitarian Universalist Community

This pamphlet was mandated by the Young Religious Unitarian Universalist Youth Council to assist youth and adults in setting boundaries and guidelines in various youth communities. It focuses primarily on overnight youth conferences, but may also be helpful in many other settings.

The District Newsletter Handbook

This resource explains how to develop a district youth newsletter.

The Fifteen-Year Review of YRUU Programs

A comprehensive review of the first fifteen years of YRUU programs at the continental, district, and local levels.

The Five Components of a Balanced Youth Program

All successful youth groups have five specific components: Worship, Community Building, Social Action, Learning, Leadership. Find out what each of these means.

The Five Steps to Building Community

This resource describes how to intentionally build community in your group by using a five-level model of sharing and opening up. This model is used in the YRUU book *Deep Fun*.

First Time Conference Attendee Packet

The basics of what one should know before attending one's first conference.

The Four Components of Successful Coming-of-Age Programs

An article from the Spring 1998 issue of *Synapse* on how to run a well-rounded Coming-of-Age program.

Fundraising in YRUU Youth Groups

Contains new and creative ideas on how to raise money for your local youth group.

A Guide to Planning a Youth Sunday

Guidelines for putting together Youth Sunday services. It is not meant to be an all-inclusive outline, but offers ideas to anyone wondering what to include in a Youth Sunday.

How to Evaluate Your YCR

This resource was created by the Resolution to Increase District and Local Participation in Youth Council (YC 1999) in order to provide a means of making sure your YCR is representing you at the continental level of YRUU.

How Do Meetings Work?

Contains general information on leadership skills, helpful hints for moderating meetings, as well a "practical guide" to consensus process.

How to Run a Successful Meeting

Some simple tricks and guidelines to run a meeting more efficiently.

How to Write YRUU Resolutions and Project Proposals

This resource was created as a way to encourage districts and local youth groups to submit resolutions for consideration at Youth Council.

JAHNNY DEPP ?

A program developed to encourage exchanges between youth governing bodies at the district level.

Learn Your ABC's

A list of commonly used UU acronyms and their definitions.

The Post-High School Survival Kit

Information for youth who are aging out of high school programs. See what is available beyond high school for youth still wanting to participate in YRUU or young adult programs.

Principles for the Establishment of Community

Learn about the principles on which community is based: respect, shared youth-adult leadership, adults, inclusiveness, sexuality, behavior rules, and enforcement of rules.

Recommended Racial Justice Action Projects

Ideas for local community and congregational anti-racism projects.

Recommended Social Action Contact List
Contact information for groups dealing with: violence, nonviolence, and gun control; AIDS and safer sex; human rights and religious liberty; reproductive rights; women's concerns; environmental concerns and animal rights; gay, lesbian, bisexual, and transgender concerns

Welcoming Lesbian, Gay, and Bisexual Youth Into YRUU
A pamphlet for youth groups.

Email Lists

The following lists are administrated by the Youth Office and open to subscription by anyone. To subscribe to any of them, go to www.uua.org/mailman/listinfo/listname where *listname* is the name of the list mentioned below.

YRUU-L: The general list for YRUUers and their allies

ADVISOR-L: For youth advisors

YRUUSJ: For YRUUers concerned with Social Justice issues

SYNAPSE-L: Updates about the YRUU online magazine, *Synapse*

There are also a number of district-specific email lists for YRUUers. For an index of all UUA lists, go to www.uua.org/mailman/listinfo.

Services and Trainings Offered by the Youth Office

The Youth Office offers leadership development youth advisor trainings (basic and advanced) and spirituality development trainings. For each of these progrms, it sends one youth and one adult trainer to the host location to lead a weekend-long event. Trainings can be customized in terms of both time and content to suit the target group. The sponsoring district or congregation is required to pay a travel equalization fee to the Youth Office and modest honoraria to the trainers. The district must also provide food and lodging for the train-

ers while they are at the site. For more details go to www.uua.org/YRUU/youthoffice/training.html. The *Training Planning Guide* is online at www.uua.org/YRUU/youthoffice/planguide.html.

Leadership Development Conferences (LDCs)
Small working conferences designed for youth and adult leaders. An LDC focuses on making the YRUU group mind "smarter" by helping the participants learn how to be effective leaders.

Spirituality Development Conference (SDC)
Conferences designed to bring youth and adult together to share common worship experiences, focusing on how to design effective, creative, and meaningful worship services and how to integrate spirituality more deeply into youth programming and into the daily lives of participants.

Basic Youth Advisor Training
Presents core issues, philosophies, and skills needed to advise and empower youth. This training is designed for new advisors looking for the basics, as well as seasoned advisors looking for support from their peers and new ideas to bring back to their group. Topics covered include youth empowerment, community building, balanced programming, liability issues, involvement in the congregation, and more.

Advanced Youth Advisor Training
Designed for advisors seeking UUA advisor certification. This training delves into more serious issues in youth advising, youth ministry, church staffing and structure, adolescent issues, and other relevant topics. It is our hope that this will become the prerequisite training for paid youth program directors and coordinators, as well as the model for future seminary courses on Ministry with Youth.

Anti-racism Trainings for Youth
A youth-led model of the UUA's Jubilee World training to explore issues of race, privilege, and oppression. Call the Youth Office for more information about these trainings and how to sponsor one for your youth group or district conference.

Consultations

UUA Youth Office staff are always available to consult with you. Please call, write, or email us with questions, comments, concerns, or ideas.

UUA Lifespan Faith Development Resources

For more information on any of these resources, contact your local religious educator, your district office, or the Lifespan Faith Development staff group assistant at (617) 948-4371. This staff group was previously called the Department of Religious Education.

Safety/Abuse Clearing House Packet

A packet of resources including sample policies, procedures, and contracts from UU congregations.

UU Faith Works (formerly the *REACH Packet*)

Published twice a year online. The packet always includes a number of resources and current information on youth and YRUU. Hard-copy subscriptions are available from Lifespan Faith Development staff group assistant at (617) 948-4361.